READING COMPREHENSION INSTRUCTION 1783-1987

A Review of Trends and Research

Authors

H. Alan Robinson

Vincent Faraone

Daniel R. Hittleman

Elizabeth Unruh

Editor

Jill Fitzgerald

International Reading Association

Newark, Delaware 19714

9.00 Net

Library of Congress Cataloging in Publication Data

✓ Reading comprehension instruction 1783-1987: A review of trends and research/ H. Alan Robinson, Vincent Faraone, Daniel R. Hittleman, Elizabeth Unruh [authors] Jill Fitzgerald [editor]

p. cm.

Includes bibliographical references.

1. Reading comprehension – Study and teaching.
2. Reading – Study and teaching – United States – History.

I. Robinson, H. Alan, 1921- II. Faraone, Vincent III. Hittleman, Daniel R. IV. Unruh, Elizabeth V. Fitzgerald, Jill

✓ LB1050.45.R427 1990 ✓ 89-38010
428.4'3 – dc20 CIP

✓ ISBN 0-87207-745-4

Cover design: Boni Nash
Photography: Larry Husfelt

Contents

Foreword

Most fields of study progress through three stages. In the first stage, all eyes are forward as the new field rushes ahead into uncharted terrain, struggling to develop the appurtenances and trappings of more established fields of study. Preservation and analysis of the past are ignored, sometimes for decades, as each new cohort of researchers does battle with a seemingly endless set of pressing issues.

Then, sometimes with the suddenness of a spring thunderstorm, the past is rediscovered and the second stage begins—a stage in which the pioneering work in the field is uncritically elevated to the heights of Parnassus. For reading research, this stage was reached in 1968 with the reissue of Huey's *Psychology and Pedagogy of Reading*. Exuberant with the rediscovery of Huey, Dodge, Cattell, and others, we failed to see merit in the work done later. More recently, however, reading research has entered a third and more mature stage wherein past work is observed and studied in the context of its own time, and the value of present work is gauged more objectively against the backdrop of its antecedents.

The present volume is a timely product of this third stage, joining a growing body of work that examines the methods, materials, outcomes, and technologies of past literacy practice. Its focus is the teaching of reading comprehension, and one of its many messages is that we have clearly learned much about comprehension instruction since the time of Huey, and all of this work has not occurred in the past several decades. On the other hand, the authors also find that the development of adequate experimental designs has progressed relatively slowly compared with that of other social sciences, and we still tend (particularly in journal articles) to give too little data to make replication possible and to pay too little attention to related earlier work, especially work published before 1966 when the ERIC service began.

Throughout the period covered by this book, ideas about reading comprehension and its instruction were derived primarily from prevailing psychological theory. Locke's doctrine of formal discipline, Herbart's (and James's) apperception, Thorndike's laws of association, and current notions about metacognition all have influenced pedagogical theory at one time or another and, through theory, textbooks and classroom practice. However, psychological theory never has been specific enough to guide instruction completely, so that instructional practices, in the end, generally have been more eclectic than their authors have wished to admit.

Nevertheless, many of the trends observed in this volume on comprehension instruction can be traced to developments in American psychology. For example, the shift from instruction built on external control over reader comprehension to internal reader control is an outcome, in this century, of the shift in emphasis within the field of psychology from behavioral to cognitive doctrines. And the shift from teaching comprehension subskills to teaching comprehension strategies derives from a more recent shift within cognitive psychology from studying separate components of complex skills to focusing on holistic routines and strategies.

To understand not only how reading comprehension was taught in the past, but also what influenced these teaching practices, is a complex and exhausting task, but one that is essential for building a complete understanding of literacy and literacy practices. The 573 readers, 369 research reports, 11 teaching manuals, and various secondary sources examined for the present work are part of a larger database that must be carefully cataloged and preserved so that further studies like this one can be done. We have made considerable progress in preserving the research literature but have done little to preserve the classroom materials and pedagogical guides, which in many cases remain in cluttered obscurity throughout America's libraries, archives, and historical societies. These are a major part of the heritage of reading research and reading practice; our commitment to their preservation and study should be as strong as our desire to improve the present.

Richard L. Venezky
University of Delaware

Preface

A few years ago, as chair of the International Reading Association Studies and Research Committee, Gene Jongsma formed a subcommittee (Gene, John Guthrie, John Regan, Sam Weintraub, Renee Weisberg, and me) to conceptualize and plan monographs on research in reading. That's where the idea for this monograph was born. We thought a historical perspective on American reading comprehension instruction could be garnered through analysis of documents from and about our early historical periods and from analysis of research on reading comprehension instruction over the years. Such a historical perspective could help teachers and researchers to better understand what we know, perceive how our knowledge has changed shape over the years, and perhaps gain keener insight into what we might do to direct the shape of the future. We knew from the start that the undertaking would be overwhelming. But we also knew that, entrusted to the able hands and thoughtful mind of senior author H. Alan Robinson, a significant monograph would be woven out of a morass of materials and reports.

This monograph takes a distinctive and vital place in a growing body of literature on the history of American reading instruction and research. It makes a special mark partly because it spotlights reading comprehension instruction, a salient contemporary focus among practitioners and researchers alike. It also makes an important mark partly because the authors insightfully interpret and synthesize work on reading comprehension instruction, forming models and making inferences about instructional notions held by people of the time. Informative and interesting portrayals are drawn of the evolving American outlook. Further, the summaries of research in Appendix A provide a record that could serve as an excellent resource for other researchers or reviewers of reading comprehension instruction.

I am grateful to the authors of this monograph for their perseverance and ability to either impose order on or extract order from piles of printed materials arrayed in chaos. Their efforts will serve many readers well for years to come.

JF

Acknowledgements

The authors wish to thank a number of people for their tremendous assistance during the preparation of this monograph. Nancy Herb facilitated the work of Vincent Faraone, who was responsible for all of the research, analysis, and writing of the second chapter. Robert Pehrsson, with the aid of his students, located and summarized many of the reports in the third chapter. The following, while graduate students at Hofstra University, located and summarized many of the reports included in this same chapter: Beth Blau, Judith Goldstein, Jim McGerald, and Bonnie Uslianer. Lynn Freed and Kim Louise Parlante, while serving as student aides, were extremely efficient and helpful in reproducing hundreds of reports for the reviewers to consider. And, as always, Marsha Regan, Alan Robinson's secretary, is applauded by all for her organized, effective, and efficient assistance—done so willingly.

We are particularly grateful to Jill Fitzgerald, our official editor—but also in many respects a collaborator—for her support over the years it has taken us to finally "put it all together." She offered help throughout the process and was never discouraged even when one or more of the authors had to turn away from the project for a period of time. She painstakingly reviewed our efforts and offered insightful criticism and suggestions for improvement. She carefully edited each part of the manuscript and was especially helpful in dealing with the detailed data in the second chapter. We are grateful, too, for the insights added to ours in the writing of the fourth chapter. The monograph is a better contribution because of Jill's scholarly input. Most of all, she provided a scaffolding that, hallelujah, helped us bring the task to its conclusion.

HAR DRH
VF EU

Contributors

Vincent Faraone
Long Island University
C.W. Post Campus
Greenvale, New York

Jill Fitzgerald
University of North Carolina at Chapel Hill
Chapel Hill, North Carolina

Daniel R. Hittleman
Queens College
City University of New York
Flushing, New York

H. Alan Robinson
Hofstra University
Hempstead, New York

Elizabeth Unruh
Hofstra University
Hempstead, New York

1

Introduction

Many contemporary theorists and researchers lament the chasm between research results and reading instruction. Venezky (1984) called for more interaction among researchers, teachers, and curriculum developers in order to affect "the practical side of reading" (p. 28). In reviewing the reading research of the 1970s, Pearson (1982) stated that although "our knowledge about the basic cognitive processes involved in reading comprehension...[and]...about basic instructional processes grew dramatically...our knowledge about teaching reading comprehension advanced very little, if at all" (p. 1).

This monograph was undertaken to learn about the nature of reading comprehension instruction in America through a study of published texts in the "preresearch" period (1783-1910), as well as published research reports from 1910 through 1987. We hoped such a survey might, in addition, provide some insights into *why* we seem to know so little today. Part of the lack of knowledge may be linked to hazy, yet persistent, notions about instruction in general and instruction in reading comprehension in particular.

We accepted as reading comprehension instruction anything an author/researcher stated or implied it to be. Definitions of reading comprehension instruction over the years have been vague and varied, to say the least. As Durkin (1979) indicated in a review of the literature for her important observational study, the attempt to find clear definitions "was non-productive."

Although investigators who focused on reading comprehension instruction across the years frequently did not state explicit definitions, implicit definitions abounded. We accepted a range of definitions when it was clear that the intent of the researcher, in a given study, was to improve or find ways of improving reading comprehension. Examples of divergent views ranged from Tovey's (1976) position that "comprehension cannot be taught directly, but situations can be provided to facilitate and encourage the processing of print into meaning" (p. 289) to Durkin's definition, that the "teacher does/says something to help children understand or work out the meaning of more than a single, isolated word" (p. 488).

Obviously, we cannot say that reading comprehension instruction as we painted it was going on in classrooms across the country. We do not know the influence textbooks and research reports had on actual teaching. We did not include theses and dissertations (unless they were published and hence available in the William S. Gray Research Collection in Reading), unpublished studies sponsored by private and public agencies, journal articles not included in the Gray Collection, or fugitive reports such as might be found in ERIC.

Because of our delimitations, we may have missed a number of important works focused on the teaching of reading comprehension. The reader must keep in mind that we did not include correlational and descriptive studies related to reading comprehension. The focus is on the teaching and/or improving of reading comprehension by taking some action. That action ranged from telling students to improve to assigning workbook pages to active teaching of skills or strategies and/or attempts to have students mobilize their background information as they dealt with given text structures.

In addition, a different team of reviewers might have selected works that we did not select and might have deleted some that are included in this monograph. We can say only that this is the way reading comprehension instruction appeared to be from our review of textbooks and research reports. In examining the research, we accepted for inclusion in this monograph only those studies in which some type of instruction was going on as explained above and delineated in the list of definitions at the end of this chapter. We did not include descriptions of reading comprehension or discussions of apparent comprehension improvement unless the investigator's purpose was to teach comprehension in some way and then assess the result.

We tried to be as objective as possible. We admit, however, that we have a view of reading instruction based on the application of holistic strategies to holistic text; hence, it is possible that some of our conclusions and ensuing discussions are colored by our own persuasions.

Overview of This Book

Chapters 2 and 3 present a picture of how authors and a large group of researchers viewed reading comprehension instruction across a broad spectrum of reading history. Faraone examined readers and teaching methods books published between 1783 and 1910, the period during which no research reports that were published focused on reading comprehension instruction. At first glance, the instructional materials published between 1783 and 1910 seemed devoid of any concentration on comprehension or of any theoretical notions. As Faraone studied and restudied materials, however, he noted concepts related to teaching understanding (the term *reading comprehension* was not used) and generated an interesting series of models related to the pursuit of meaning. His report and analyses are presented in Chapter 2.

Chapter 3 reflects the review of the research in the teaching of reading comprehension from 1910-1987 done by Robinson, Hittleman, and Unruh. (Actually, the first study concerned with reading comprehension instruction was not published until 1918.) Although it would have been interesting to continue the review of basic readers from 1910 on, since this is essentially a review of the research, we did not review the many readers published during this three-quarters of a century.

In Chapter 4, we have raised some questions, posed some problems, and attempted to look at future directions for both the practitioner and the researcher.

Finally, a review of all the studies focused on reading comprehension instruction examined in thc preparation of this monograph is included in Appendix A, followed by an alphabetical listing by author of each study in Appendix B.

Our definitions of reading comprehension instruction represent the various implicit notions about reading comprehension instruction used across the years. Some are current; others are true only of certain time periods. For example, numbers 1 and 2 represent positions taken by early writers of basic reading books. A number of the definitions build clearly on Durkin's broad, nonspecific definition. Number 25 has begun to receive attention as knowledge of process has increased. Number 26 is more a notion than a reality, but there are indications of implementation. Number 27 seems to hold promise, at least for students in the middle school and above, although there are few published studies that demonstrate the results of instruction focused on self-monitoring as a means of improving reading comprehension.

Implied Definitions of Reading Comprehension Instruction

1. Teach pupils to sound out letters, put them together as words, and understanding will take place automatically.

2. Have pupils memorize words, put them together in sentences, and understanding will take place automatically.

3. Have students read silently, and comprehension will improve.

4. Present material relevant to the life experience, language knowledge, and/or interests of the learners, and comprehension will take place.

5. Have learners read text they created, and comprehension will be automatic.

6. Encourage and urge learners to read with understanding, and comprehension will occur.

7. Diagnose the problems of readers, remind them of such problems as they undertake a reading task, encourage them to be aware of their problems as they read, and better comprehension will take place.

8. Administer standardized or informal tests frequently, and the readers' comprehension will improve.

9. Have learners graph their progress across a set of materials, and their comprehension will improve.

10. Use drill materials with items that are similar to items on tests being used in order to improve comprehension.

11. Drill readers on a set of comprehension skills (usually derived through authoritative opinion), and understanding will improve.

12. Discuss the learners' weaknesses (and sometimes strengths) in classes, groups, or in individual conferences as a means of stimulating increased comprehension.

13. Have learners read out loud, ask them questions about their reading, and correct their errors during reading in order to improve comprehension.

14. Have learners read material silently and ask a series of questions about the material. With such repeated questioning, comprehension will improve.

15. Put time on task, that is, be sure learners get enough opportunities to read in unbroken segments of time. This may include class time reading silently and/or orally for a given task or independent silent reading. Comprehension will increase.

16. Concentrate on one specific skill (e.g., main idea) or strategy (e.g., SQ3R) in order to improve comprehension.

17. Use a teaching plan, such as the directed reading activity (DRA), to stimulate and improve comprehension.

18. Provide simulated or life experiences related to the text to be read, and comprehension will be enhanced.

19. Present or develop with the learners purposes for reading in order to facilitate comprehension.

20. Discuss important words in the reading assignment before the reading takes place, and comprehension will improve.

21. Brainstorm in some way prior to reading using oral discussion, prereading questions, outlining, visual or audiovisual presentations, or mapping—and comprehension will improve.

22. Insert or raise questions to be answered during the reading to increase comprehension.

23. Offer monetary rewards in advance of silent reading to improve reading comprehension.

24. Use postorganizers to improve comprehension, such as groups of related questions, outlining, paraphrasing, or mapping.

25. Break down the components of a strategy—such as summarizing—and carefully teach, in a direct fashion, each component. Follow the process with practice of the strategy, and comprehension will increase.

26. Teach a skill or strategy, furnish guided and independent practice, and then present and guide the application of the skill or

strategy in another context; that is, ensure transfer in order to improve comprehension.

27. To improve reading comprehension, raise the learner's consciousness – mobilize self-monitoring – of methods employed in reading or studying.

References

Durkin, D. What classroom observations reveal about reading comprehension instruction. *Reading Research Quarterly,* 1979, *14,* 481-533.

Pearson, P.D. *A context for instructional research on reading comprehension.* Urbana, IL: Center for the Study of Reading, University of Illinois, 1982.

Tovey, D. Improving children's comprehension abilities. *The Reading Teacher,* 1976, *30,* 288-292.

Venezky, R.L. The history of reading research. In P.D. Pearson (Ed.), *Handbook of reading research.* New York: Longman, 1984.

2

Reading Comprehension Instruction in America: 1783-1910

In this chapter, reading comprehension instruction in the United States from 1783 to 1910 is portrayed—prior to the impact of reading research on instructional practices in American schools. Two specific questions are addressed: (1) What perceptions of the reading process or models of reading predominated during the period 1783-1910? and (2) What notions about facilitating reading comprehension were held by American educators prior to 1910?

The dates 1783-1910 were selected for two reasons: (1) 1783 marked the publication of Noah Webster's *Grammatical Institute of the English Language, Part 1*. While this speller confirmed an ancient tradition in teaching reading, it was the first experimentation in reading education in the postrevolutionary period and a harbinger of the emerging influence of the school reader as an experimental tool in classroom instruction. (2) The cutoff date, 1910, was suggested by the research of Smith (1965, 1986) and Guthrie (1984), both of whom observed that research findings began to have practical application to classroom instruction after 1910.

The term *model* as used in question 1 signified "a structure or design to show how something (i.e., reading) is formed or how it functions, by analyzing thc rclationships of its various parts to each other and to the whole" (Harris & Hodges, 1981, p. 200). The term *notions* was used in question 2 to signify hypotheses or workable assumptions for classroom practice.

Method of Study

Sources

Primary sources investigated were limited to books used for reading instruction. There were 585 primary sources surveyed, the majority of which (573) were readers published from 1783-1910. The remaining sources were books and periodicals written for teachers on educational theory and practices (Arnold, 1894, 1899; Carter, 1829a, 1829b; Chubb, c1902; Davis, 1839; Farnham, 1895; Hall, 1829; Keagy, 1826; Moore, 1909; Parker, c1883; Wickersham, c1865). The secondary sources were Diack (1965), Guthrie (1984), Johnson (1917), Kline, Moore, and Moore (1987), Marrou (1948), Mathews (1966), Perkinson (1985), Reeder (1900), Robinson (1930), Smith (1965, 1986), Tuer (1896), Venezky (1987), and Westerhoff (1978).

Innovative classroom practices in reading comprehension from 1783 to 1910 most likely occurred through teacher use of the reading textbook (Perkinson, 1985; Venezky, 1987). These textbooks were, in a sense, experimental tools used by author-educators to test certain notions related to problems of reading instruction. A common practice was for authors to comment on the merits of their innovative approaches in the prefaces of their readers, some with claims that they were based on practical classroom experiences. For example, Town (1846), a popular author of children's readers, wrote that his reading lessons were "in strict accordance with experimental results" based on information obtained "from several County Institutes [for teacher training] and...some hundreds of practical teachers of large experience" (p. 5). Although Town's comment was probably intended to increase the sale of his readers, it also explicitly supported the importance of experimenting with instructional materials in reading through field testing—a practice reported by several nineteenth century author-educators.

Procedure

Content analysis of the texts was accomplished using the following procedure. First, school readers—defined as any "book used for instruction in reading" (Harris & Hodges, 1981, p. 263)—were examined for explicit statements made by author-educators related to reading comprehension. These statements most often were found in the preface of the text or in a special section addressed to the attention of teachers. Second, when an explicit statement was observed, the text was further examined to locate text variables in the reader, or among the author's teaching suggestions, that supported the observed statement. A text variable was defined as any feature of a reader intended by the author for a specific instructional purpose. Features as widely different as typography, pictures, questions printed in the text, literary format, and a glossary were all considered text variables (see Table 1, pp. 36-39). Third, the explicit statements observed in the readers with their text variables were then categorized into notions related to reading comprehension. Fourth, models of the reading process were inferred from the notions observed.

Preview of Findings

Three distinct time periods emerged as a result of the investigation that showed an early nineteenth century view of reading (prior to 1826) as a facilitator and caretaker of memory; a midnineteenth century view of reading (1826-1882) as an expressive art; and a turn of the century view (1883-1910) that regarded reading as a receptive process. In the sections that follow, each of these time periods is developed around (1) inferred models of the reading process as perceived by author-educators of the time; (2) the notions or hypotheses they appear to be based on related to reading comprehension instruction; and (3) the ways author-educators tested these notions in the texts they designed for reading instruction through the use of selected text variables and the comprehension activities they suggested for classroom practice.

Some initial clarifying remarks are needed about terms. First, it became evident as this study progressed that reading educators prior to 1910 did not clearly differentiate between reading comprehension as a process or as a product. They used a variety of expressions to refer to *reading comprehension*, a term that had not yet come into educational vogue. Some of their terms suggested process (e.g., searching out what is truth, exercising the reflective power) and some suggested product (e.g., imbibing the feelings of the author, acquiring the signification).

Second, the expressions they did use clearly associated reading comprehension with both cognitive and affective dimensions. For example, in defining "reading [comprehension] as a mental operation," Wickersham (c1865) related it to both intellect and emotions. He stated, "Unless there are intellects to think and hearts to feel there can be no good reading" (p. 220). The most popular term used in the nineteenth century was, perhaps, *intellectual reading*.

Third, as used by nineteenth century author-educators in their writings, the more generic term *reading* was synonomous with *oral reading*.Although these writers did distinguish between *silent* reading and *loud* reading (Cobb, c1831, 1833; Staniford, c1815, 1817), they considered the reading process incomplete unless it culminated in expressive reading. Fourth, no clear distinction was made between the reading processes of the child or "little adult" and the mature adult reader. They believed that both children and adults went through similar steps in order to read and while reading. What distinguished the child from the adult was simply age and experience and the difficulty level of the materials used. The process of reading for children and adults differed mostly in degree, not in substance.

Finally, in contrast to *reading*, the word *study* meant reading and rereading text with close attention. This activity invariably implied silent reading or reading quietly (subvocalizing) to one's self. The child who had not mastered the mechanics of the text could be made to study or attend to text through ongoing supervision by the teacher or an older student.

The Memoriter Model: An Early View of the Reading Process (prior to 1826)

When Noah Webster published his speller in 1783, he was perpetuating a view of the reading process—as well as a procedure for teaching it—that was basically unchanged from the time it first appeared in ancient Greece. This view was inextricably bound to the alphabetic writing system the Greeks had perfected (Mathews,

1966). They believed that writing was a means to capture the human voice using a system of silent symbolic notations. The process of reading, and learning to read, was simply a way to recapture that voice in the same orderly manner used by the creator of the text. That orderly manner, Greek logic dictated, was a synthetic process beginning with letter names, building into syllables, then words, then sentences, and finally whole text (Marrou, 1948). The oral recitation of the writer's text (voice) was a confirmation that reading had occurred. If one repeated this process often enough with the same text, then the voice captured in that text also could be captured in one's own memory.

In the America of Noah Webster and his colonial predecessors, the objective of "capturing the voice of the writer in one's own memory" took on special significance, especially with text of inestimable value, such as religious and scholarly writings. Since books were scarce and the written word was not always available for the potential reader, children memorized prayers and catechetical responses, adults memorized psalms set to verse and other biblical selections, and scholars memorized learned treatises.

Reading, in a sense, was looked upon as a facilitator and caretaker of memory – a process that consisted of separate, yet mutually dependent hierarchical levels (see Figure 1). Lower levels of reading supported higher levels, while at the same time higher levels of reading reinforced lower levels. For example, successful oral reading of text (Stage 3) was dependent upon complete familiarity with the text (Stage 2) and its words and word components (Stage 1). Conversely, successful oral reading of the text reinforced memory of the text and the word and word components associated with it.

The secular version of the view of reading shown in Figure 1 appeared in the preface of Staniford's *The Art of Reading* (c1815, 1817, pp. 9-10) and over a decade later – word for word unchanged – in Cobb's *Third Juvenile Reader* (c1831, 1833, p. xiii), in which they wrote:

> The principal objects to be obtained by reading are three: 1. to acquire knowledge; 2. to assist the memory to attain the knowledge when acquired; and 3. to communicate it to

Figure 1
The Memoriter Model (Prior to 1826)
Reading as a Facilitator and Caretaker of Memory

Religious View		Secular View
3. The Word of God, once obtained, was communicated to others. The ability to communicate the Word of God was the final stage in reading.	3. Oral reading of the text.	3. Knowledge, once acquired, was shared with others. The ability to communicate knowledge was the hallmark of an enlightened mind and the final stage in reading.
2. The Word of God was committed to memory through repetitive drills and/or meditation of the text, i.e., silent reading.	2. Rote memorization of the text through silent reading.	2. Knowledge was preserved in memory through repetitive drills and/or reflective study.
1. Spelling, i.e., decoding, and pronunciation, i.e., acquiring a sight vocabulary, were the keys that unlocked the Word of God, i.e., the meaning of the text.	1. Spelling, pronunciation, and defining to unlock the meaning of the text.	1. Spelling, pronunciation, and defining were the means through which the reader acquired knowledge, i.e., the meaning of the text.

> others. The first two are answered by silent reading; but to communicate knowledge to others loud reading is necessary.

Although this citation makes no reference to spelling and pronunciation, Staniford and Cobb and their contemporaries required this practice with all new words in their readers prior to oral recitation. They also assumed that, prior to the introduction of the reader, the child had been thoroughly instructed in a speller, or a primer.

Memoriter Notions on Teaching Reading Comprehension

The view of reading, as shown in the memoriter model, was supported by several notions related to the teaching of reading comprehension.

1. Meaningful text (i.e., one that communicated a message) was delayed in beginning reading instruction until decoding was mastered. In the preface of an American reprint of Dilworth's speller (1807), this notion is expressed quite clearly:

> Until children be grounded in the knowledge of letters and syllables, their attention should be engaged in considering the structure of words without regard to their meaning.... It is unreasonable to expect that persons who cannot pronounce the letters should perceive the idea expressed by it; much less can it be expected that they should comprehend the meaning of phrases or sentences (pp. v-vi).

Webster (1783), for example, placed his first reading lessons for young children at the end of his speller, after countless lists of words. It was an apparent reminder to teachers not to begin reading until children had learned their spellings. It was during this period that the speller had its greatest popularity as an instructional tool in reading.

2. The comprehensible text for the learner was decodable text. The logic of the alphabet approach dictated that word difficulty increased as the numbers of letters or syllables in the word increased; therefore, reading vocabulary in primary reading lessons was controlled on this basis. *The Tract Primer* (1848), a vestige of this period, began its first reading lessons with these two letter words that then increased to three:

Is he up to us? No.
Woe be to me if it is so (p. 16).

God can see all men.
Who can see God? Not one.
You may not sin for God can see you (p. 18).

However, this practice was not observed beyond the primary level since content of more advanced readers was primarily a compilation of religious, moralistic, didactic, and oratorical selections "better calculated for such as have *learned* than those who are learning to read" (Strong, 1824, p. 5). Leavitt (c1847, 1852) made a similar observation about earlier readers:

> Many compilers seemed to have merely followed their own literary tastes in making their selections. They have filled their books with choice and elegant extracts, valuable indeed as materials for a scrap-book but quite above the level of children's minds, and not chosen with any special reference to their appropriateness as exercises in reading (p. iii).

Leavitt's criticism was indeed correct. Gradation as a practice of rendering text more comprehensible to the reader was restricted to primary reading materials since it was assumed that older students had mastered their spellings. The term *gradation* meant gradually increasing the number of letters and/or syllables in the words of the child's first reading materials, as well as gradually increasing sentence length. It was also applied to the practice of author-educators who were experimenting with series readers that increased in reading difficulty, a practice not fully appreciated by some. Hall (c1836, 1837) observed that "it would be idle to think of providing a separate reading book for each of [the] grades; any attempt to graduate books to their respective wants, would produce complexity and confusion, rather than any real advantage" (p. iii).

3. The acquisition of a sight vocabulary, through efficient rapid decoding, automatically facilitated the acquisition of meaning. In 1824, Leavitt complained that "children are put forth too fast in their reading. They should be kept in their spellings until they can

readily pronounce common words at sight" (p. 6). The acquisition of a sight vocabulary apparently was tantamount to the acquisition of meaning. Willard (1828) expanded further on this notion:

> The first elements of reading...consist of those words-...familiar to the ears, tongues, and understandings of children before they are old enough to hold a book....These common words are...to be made familiar to the eyes of the learner, so that he may readily read them in composition. After this they should be employed as a means of acquainting him with the signification of other words while he is learning the orthography and pronunciation of them (p. iv).

4. Use of the dictionary facilitated decoding as well as the acquisition of meaning. Adams (c1819, 1821) advised the schoolmasters of his day, "Let the student be taught, while studying his lesson, ever to have his dictionary within reach of him" (p. iii). He presented in the margin of his reader a column of words to be studied and defined by students. Dictionaries, however, were not always available to all; therefore, the practice increased of including word definitions in spellers and readers. The practice assisted not only students but also the untrained and poorly educated teachers who were often employed by schools in postrevolutionary America. This period culminated with the publication of Webster's (1828) dictionary.

5. Rote memorization of text facilitated the acquisition of meaning. In 1815, Staniford wrote that one of "the principal objects to be attained by reading [is] to assist the memory to retain this knowledge when acquired" (p. 9). The assumption was that if learners could memorize major portions of content, they had mastered the meaning of that content, if not at that time, at least for future use. Memory, in this sense, was considered not only a preserver but also an incubator of meaning. Leonard (c1825, 1827) wrote:

> The grand object "aimed at" is that while the pupil reads his daily lesson he shall not only learn to pronounce words, but shall also treasure up a valuable stock of ideas, to enlarge his mind, to interest his heart, and to prepare him for his future scenes on the theatre of life (p. v).

In fact, some of the readers of this period took on the appearance of a secular catechism using a question-answer format so that content would "more easily be committed to memory and better understood" (Strong, c1819, 1822, preface). For example, the opening pages of *Cobb's Spelling Book* (c1825, 1831) began with a 12 page catechism of the "Rudiments of the English Language" containing 90 questions (Q) followed by answers (A) which were to be memorized by students:

> Q. What are *letters?*
> A. *Letters* are the marks of sounds, and the rudiments of *written Language* which are presented to the eye.
> Q. What is *written Language?*
> A. It is composed of *letters, syllables,* and *words,* which represent *articulate sounds* (p. 6).

One hundred years later, Johnson (1917) commented on this practice, observing that "precepts were instilled in minds as yet unformed, and the children were drilled to believe what they were to think out for themselves when they were more mature" (p. 70).

6. Study (i.e., the acquisition of meaning through silent reading and rereading) was the sole responsibility of the scholar—the older student. The preoccupation of the teacher in both primary and advanced classes was oral recitation, especially with "rules and exercises in correct pronunciation and enunciation" (Smith, 1965, 1986, p. 38). No system of practices had yet been developed by reading educators at this time to support the scholar's efforts to study, other than sheer memorization of content, use of the dictionary, and random questioning by the schoolmaster. Study was deemed the province of the older student, not the child in the primary stages of reading. Its major purpose was to reinforce reading memory, as well as meaning, in order to prepare the student for the final stage of reading—effective oral communication of text.

7. The ability to communicate the written text effectively through oral reading indicated that the reader had mastered the meaning of the text. This was a major activity and the final goal of reading instruction in the advanced classes of American schools

during this period. The concern with effective oral communication of text seemed eminently suited for a new nation that wished to safeguard freedoms of the "pulpit" as well as the "public forum." New readers reflected this concern, containing the words *orator* and *speaker* in their titles (Barbauld, 1824; Bingham, 1815; Cooke, 1814; Putnam, 1836). Dickinson (1821) observed that "the art of reading well consists in conveying to the hearer the whole meaning of the writer" (p. x). However, for this to occur, he maintained that "the subject must first operate upon the reader or speaker, before he can operate upon the subject" (p. xi); i.e., the text first must be understood by the reader, before he or she can communicate the text.

The Spelling Method: Exemplar of Memoriter-Repetitional Instruction

The instructional approach used in colonial America was the ancient alphabet or spelling method of the Greeks, which already had been in use in England for several centuries with the introduction of the hornbook (Tuer, 1896). The method reappeared in post-revolutionary America, considerably expanded and updated in several spellers, but notably in Webster's *Grammatical Institute of the English Language, Part 1* (1783). Marrou's (1948) description of the reading lesson in Hellenistic schools could well apply to the practices occurring in the classrooms of Webster's day. The similarity in methodology was extraordinary:

> [The Hellenistic] method was based on a purely rational *a priori* analysis of the thing to be learnt, in complete indifference to the learner's–i.e., the child's psychological problems. Learning proceeded from the simple to the complex, from part to the whole....Any other procedure would have seemed absurd–as it seemed later to St. Augustine. Hence, the first thing to be learned was the alphabet, then syllables, then words, then sentences, and finally continuous passages. One stage was not tackled until all the problems in the preceding stage had been fully dealt with–which meant spending a long time on each (p. 150).

Smith (1965, 1986) described the spelling method as "the memoriter repetitional method of learning to read" (p. 73), since the central, unchanging activity of the child's school day in a colonial and early nineteenth century classroom was marked by emphasis on memorization (memoriter) and drill (repetitional). The steps involved in the spelling method follow.

1. *Spelling, pronouncing, and defining.* Primary classes were initiated into reading by first learning the alphabet and then spelling long lists of syllables and words that were committed to memory. The most popular text used for instruction was the speller, followed by the primary reader. Their initial pages invariably contained the alphabet, a syllabarium, and lists of spelling words that increased progressively in number of syllables. Young children spent most of the school day spelling and memorizing; they remained at this stage until instruction in reading selections began. In his *Lectures on School Reading,* Hall (1829) advised teachers: "Spelling is important and should take up a great part of your day" (p. 82). This was apparently standard practice in American schools as late as 1847 for, appearing in the *Statutes of the State of New York Relating to Common Schools* (Benton, 1847), there were requirements for town superintendents to file a comprehensive report with the county clerk that included the following information related to "the course and extent of study pursued" [in reading]:

> Number of pupils learning the alphabet.
> Number of pupils learning to spell without being able to read.
> Number of pupils learning to read.
> [Number of pupils learning] to define words (pp. 183-184).

This practice was still popular after the Civil War (Wickersham, c1865) and continued as an alternative mode of teaching in some primers as late as 1893 (Sanders, c1866, 1893).

Once a sight vocabulary was established, pupils prepared for the recitation (Stage 3) by studying the text (Stage 2) and by "spelling their way through their sentences." Older pupils were required to recite the memorized definitions of new words. If pupils faltered on a word, they were instructed to spell it out to assist them in solving the unknown word.

2. *Rote memorization of text.* Reading selections were read by the teacher, repeated by the class, and, after many repetitions,

drilled into memory. This procedure was particularly necessary for younger children who needed direct teacher supervision in order to attend to the text, since they had not fully mastered their spellings or a sight vocabulary. The teacher's oral reading served as a model preparation for the recitation to come. In the preface of his reader, Alden (c1802, 1822) advised teachers:

> The instructer [sic] must have an accurate ear and be capable of modulating his voice; and it must be his business to make the learner take the tones from him. No one who is not thus qualified ought ever to attempt to teach reading (p. iv).

Students in the upper grades were instructed to study lessons on their own in order to memorize content and prepare for the oral recitation. Dictionary usage was required by some teachers when meanings of new words proved to be illusive. Study, if provided by the teacher in the schoolroom, was the only time silent reading occurred in the class, a goal never achieved by some students who continued to vocalize every word quietly to themselves.

3. *Oral reading of text.* Oral reading proceeded according to certain rules established by the teacher or the author of the reader being used. Hall (1829, pp. 84-85) cited these representative rules for a successful recitation period:

> (a) When a class is reading, no one has leave to ask a question or to change his place; (b) require every scholar to pronounce every syllable distinctly...; (c) be careful to show every scholar the importance and use of the stops or points in reading, and require them to observe them; and (d) be careful to lead the attention of the class to the character of the lesson to be read, and to make the manner and tone of voice correspond to it.

Diack (1965) contended that the alphabet method, as explained in Stage 1 and as introduced in colonial America via the hornbook and early primer, was not a pure spelling method:

> Even the diligent student of the history of reading is likely to get the impression from books on this subject that the

> pupil who was taught by an alphabetic method learned the names of the letters but not their sounds. This misconception arises from the anxiety of writers on this subject to distinguish between phonic (sounding) methods and alphabetic methods. They emphasize that in alphabetic methods the names of the letters were given and that in phonic methods the sounds of the letters were given and omit to point out that the teaching material of the simple hornbook, to say nothing of the early primer, was designed quite precisely for the purpose of teaching the sounds of consonants when combined with vowels (p. 12).

Diack was correct if he meant that students who memorized the teaching material of the syllabarium likewise learned a combination of consonant and vowel sounds as wholes (e.g., ab, ac, ad). However, nineteenth century author-educators, who witnessed both methods, made a very clear distinction between alphabetic and phonic approaches: A phonic approach taught specific letter-sound correspondence. Tower (c1853), a phonic supporter in his day, instructed teachers that "the pupil, in spelling should often give the powers [sounds] of the several elements of words, instead of merely naming the letters" (p. 9). And, as late as 1881, *Sheldon & Co's. Modern School First Reader* stated: "the alphabetic or a,b,c method begins by teaching the *forms* and *names* of the letters, without reference to their sounds when found in words" (p. iv). The description of the spelling approach appearing in this chapter makes no assumption of sounding procedures.

The Interlocking and Step by Step Models: A Mid-Nineteenth Century View of Reading (1826 to 1882)

The year 1826 heralded the publication in Boston of *The American Journal of Education,* which became a forum for American educators at a time when they were beginning to evaluate past practices in reading instruction and experiment with innovative approaches. Articles appeared in this journal from educators extolling Pestalozzian concepts in education and questioning reading practices that were not meaningful to children. Memoriter instructional practices in reading, and the spelling method in particular, came under severe criticism. Keagy (1826) referred to the spelling book as "the greatest barrier now existing to [the child's] intellectual improvement [i.e., development of reading comprehension] (p. 673)." An unsigned article entitled "Interrogatory Instruction," probably written by the editor, James Carter (1829a), made this reference to the catechetical approach:

> [This] method of instruction...has...a tendency to deaden rather than to enliven the mind, and to confine rather than to extend its inquiries. The questions proposed in most books...usually *assume* the point at which the learner ought to arrive by his own investigation, and what is still worse, that the answers to the interrogation put into the mouth of the teacher are not left to flow from the scholar's own mind, but are very carefully and minutely printed off beforehand in order to save him, as it were, the trouble and the very possibility of thinking at all (p. 142).

In a later article, Carter (1829b) continued his criticism of memoriter learning:

> Too much of our effort has hitherto been expended in loading the *memory,* to the partial or total neglect of the other faculties....As for treasuring up in the memory for *future* years that which we cannot now understand, it is a great error. Nothing should ever be taught a child but what he can see the utility of, in a greater or less degree and reduce to practice (p. 387).

Similar criticisms also began to appear in the prefaces of newly published readers. Willard (1828) wrote an attack on spellers in which he concluded: "The objections stated lie perhaps in nearly equal degrees to all spelling books, which have attracted much attention for these forty or fifty years." His strongest objection was "against the usual practice of making orthography and pronunciation the sole business of children in the commencement of their studies" (p. v), a business that Merriam (1829) complained led to "the monotonous drawl so frequently heard in the reading of school boys" (p. iv). Pierpont (c1830, 1833) likewise derided the spelling method, observing that students should exercise themselves "with words that are drawn together by *sense,* rather than by sound, and are addressed not to the eye only, but to the *mind*."

Morley (c1838, 1839) not only attacked the early practices of the spelling method, but also the effects the memoriter repetitional method of learning to read had on older students. He summed up the criticism of the day in this statement:

> Children and youth are taught to spell and read what they do not understand, to define without understanding the definitions, and to commit to memory the words of grammar, rhetoric, geography, history, philosophy, logic...while scarcely a sentence is understood (p. iv).

The Interlocking Model of the Reading Process

An emerging perception of reading was expressed by Davis (1839) in his teaching methods book. In an initial discussion of spelling, pronunciation, and defining, he abandoned the "common mode" of beginning reading instruction (i.e., the spelling method) in favor of the "new mode" as exemplified by Gallaudet's and Bumstead's assessment of the elementary education of children—it was devoid of meaning.

Their new mode involved the introduction of a sight vocabulary (sometimes with pictures) followed by learning of the letter names and the beginning of oral reading of simple stories as soon as a small reservoir of words had been mastered. Davis's reference to Gallaudet (c1835, 1839) included this quotation from Gallaudet's *The Mother's Primer*:

> In the common modes what can be more uninteresting than to commence with teaching a child to call *certain arbitrary marks*, or letters, which in themselves have no meaning, by *certain arbitrary sounds*, or names of the letters which have no meaning. What an unintelligible and irksome task it must be (p. 6).

After this discussion of the new mode, Davis then devoted an entire chapter to a new synthesis of reading:

> Reading may be taught as a *mechanical,* as an *intellectual,* or as a *rhetorical* exercise....The *mechanical* part of reading consists in the modulation of the voice as to loudness, distinctness of articulation, and slowness, and in regard to propriety of pronunciation, emphasis, tones, and pauses ....The *intellectual* part of reading is the most important and the most difficult. It consists in teaching children to understand what they read....Let them understand that the object of reading is very different from the object aimed at in jumping rope; that it is not for exercise, but to cull and collect the writer's thoughts and to preserve them for future use....The *rhetorical* part of reading consists chiefly in entering into the spirit of the author so as to imbibe his temper and feelings [that is to] read with force, variety, and if necessary, with deep emotion (pp. 45-49).

Although Davis's synthesis retained the three obvious stages of its progenitor – the memoriter model – its emphases were clearly different. His model, with its initial support of the new mode of teaching, gave a central role to meaning in learning to read and highlighted the importance of silent reading comprehension. It questioned the validity of reading memory as sheer repetition of the text without giving the sense of the text. It also recognized the need to begin focusing on reading comprehension early in the child's reading development (see Figure 2).

In Davis's model, mastery of all three stages of reading was facilitated by meaning – in a sense, the keystone or interlocking piece that made the entire process work. Preparation for the meaning of the text not only assisted in one's mastery of the mechanics of reading, but also enabled the reader to comprehend the text through independent silent reading, culminating eventually in expressive reading – the final goal of the reading act. Some of Davis's contemporaries even claimed that meaning at the first stage was crucial, for without it "reading without thinking" would develop. Olney (c1833, 1839) wrote:

Figure 2
The Interlocking Model (1826-1882)
Reading as an Expressive Art

3. Achieving meaning naturally led to the successful communication of the writer's message.

2. This preparation enabled the reader to achieve the text's meaning through independent study, i.e., silent reading.

1. Preparation for the meaning of the text aided one's competency in the mechanics of reading.

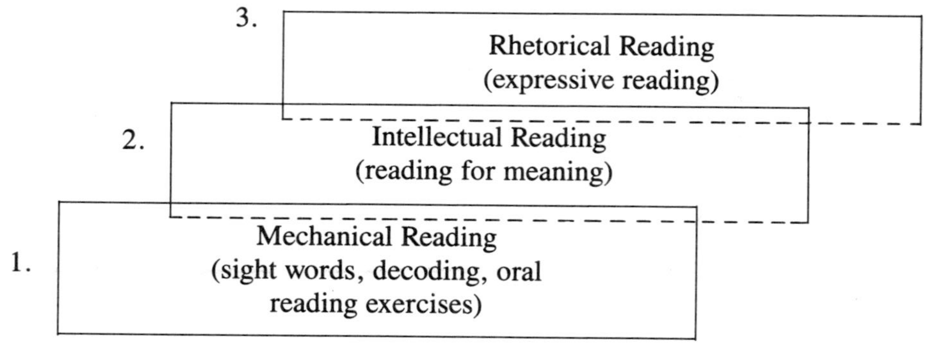

> Let a pupil, six or seven years of age, be permitted to read two or three years, in a careless unthinking manner—hurrying over sentences without understanding them—attaching no meaning to the words that he reads, and he will contract habits of thoughtlessness, indifference and inattention ....Such a course of instruction does not lead him to *think*....Nothing can be a greater obstacle to the acquisition of vigorous investigation, and of sound and useful knowledge, than the habit of *reading without thinking*...(p. 3).

Bumstead (c1852, 1859) later wrote that the habit of nonthinking started earlier, prior to mechanical oral reading exercises, with drills in "the fragments of words" appearing in the syllabarium. "Such lessons...are as unnecessary as they are uninteresting; conveying no thought, but rather teaching a child *not* to think" (p. 3).

The view held by Davis was reflected in a number of series readers published, in particular for the primary classes. Lovell (c1836, 1852) recommended the use of the explanatory mode as an instructional practice beginning with his first reader, as did McGuffey (1836) and Webb (1862), who included questions in their texts after each reading selection. The term *explanatory mode* refers to an instructional procedure that required students to explain the text based on questions asked by the teacher during the recitation period. An early and detailed discussion of "the explanatory system of instruction" can be found in Emerson's *The First-Class Reader* (c1833, 1836, pp. 9-14).

Webb's readers at each level clearly stressed the central role of meaning in reading. In his *Normal Reader, Number 4* (c1850, 1853), for example, the first criterion for reading well was "a full comprehension of the matter to be read," which he recommended could be obtained through careful silent reading previous to the oral recitation. McGuffey (1837) likewise recognized the importance of meaning in reading and vigorously defended his practice of including questions in his readers as a means of going beyond the cultivation of memory to develop understanding of text.

Another author-educator who emphasized reading meaning for young readers was Sargent, whose first reader (c1860, 1866) included for study the introduction of new words, with written definitions, prior to the reading lesson – a practice that was widely used only in more advanced readers. However, the best examples of the interweaving of meaning and mechanics in a reader for very young children were the object method primers that became popular after the 1880s. These colorful books, with their emphasis on picture learning, developed words, phrases, or short sentences beginning with the presentation of concrete experiences (i.e., objects or acts) to children (Crosby, 1896; Kirk, 1899; Taylor, c1895; Wooster, 1899).

The interlocking model clearly recognized the central role of meaning in reinforcing mechanics, as well as expressive reading. It acknowledged, in a sense, the reading process as triune, i.e., consisting of three distinct but interdependent elements with reading meaning as its keystone.

The Step-by-Step Model of the Reading Process

Around the time Davis wrote his synthesis of reading, several author-educators had become interested in studies dealing with the scientific analysis of the powers of the English language, as illustrated by Webster's monumental work, *An American Dictionary of the English Language* (1828). They recognized the potential this analysis had for the teaching of reading as they sought a rational approach that would lead the learner to a complete mastery of reading. Although these educators shared Davis's view of the importance of intellectual reading, as well as his dissatisfaction with the spelling approach, they rejected the word method as a beginning reading approach. Swan (c1844, 1847) summed up his criticism of the word method with these questions:

> What does the child acquire by this process more than the recollection of twenty-six familiar words? Has anything been learned that will enable him to pronounce the twenty-seventh word? Or has the memory alone been cultivated as by the other method [a reference to the spelling method] and by so doing he is enabled to pronounce only as many words as he can recollect from often repeating them? (p. iv)

As shown in Figure 3, the step-by-step model included the same three components as the interlocking model. In the step-by-step model, the components of reading and of learning to read occurred one step at a time. Swan (c1844, 1847) asserted, "The pronunciation of words is the *mechanical* part. This can only be taught to children successfully by first teaching them the *powers* of the letters. Teaching them that words are signs of ideas is the *intellectual* part...." (p. iii). Reading consisted of three distinct, separate hierarchical stages in which mastery of a lower stage facilitated and, indeed, was required before mastery of the next stage (see Figure 3).

Numerous educators after 1850 shared Swan's belief "in the powers of the letters" for developing competency in decoding. One special group consisted of the authors of elaborate experimental phonic approaches, such as Longley (1852), Knell (c1868), and Knudson (c1887). Although their phonic systems differed radically, they all progressed along the orderly lines of "teaching one thing at a time" and were based on a common underlying premise: Quick mastery of the mechanics of decoding initially would lead to mastery of articulation, enunciation, and, eventually, intellectual reading. Knudson, for example, was so convinced about his new system of reading that he wrote this special note "Tu the Ti'cher" in the appendix of his primer:

> The alfabet uzd is i'zili lernd, so that the pupils can su'n help themselvs in ri'ding the words, and thos gen encorejment tu go on chi'rfuli acwiring the abiliti tu enonshiet distinctli, and therbi being the foundeshon for an intelijibl pli'zing ri'ding and spi'king, hwich is so rerli met with in the English langwej (p. iii).

The theme of "teaching one thing at a time" was elaborated by Tower, author of the popular *Gradual Readers* (c1853, 1860). The unspoken motto of his series was "step-by-step." In his primer, *The Child's First Step Taken in the Right Place* (c1853), Tower introduced a new plan in beginning reading "embodying the advantages" of both the spelling and word methods and based on the knowledge of the powers of the letters. The child learned a few letters and their

Figure 3
The Step-by-Step Model (1826-1882)
Reading as an Expressive Art

3. Achieving meaning automatically assured successful communication of the writer's message.
2. The meaning of the text was achieved through independent study, i.e., silent reading, rereading.
1. Competency in the mechanics of reading was necessary before the meaning of the text was achieved.

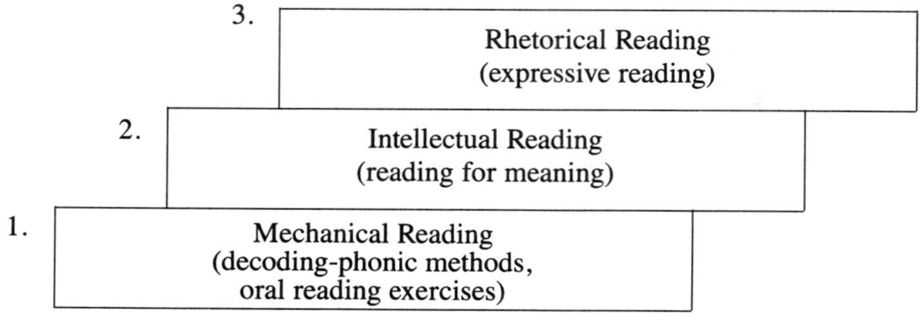

sounds before he or she read a meaningful word containing those letters. Tower's primer alternated between exercises on the powers of the letters and reading lessons of simple sentences stressing their articulation. He introduced vowel sounds first, using phonetically consistent words, and he cautioned teachers (c1845, 1852) not to proceed to the next step of reading phrases until "the pupil has learned a few of the powers of the vowels." Tower believed that correct enunciation would lead to correct decoding.

In *The Gradual Reader: First Step of Exercises in Articulation* (c1853, 1860), organized into two major sections—exercises and reading lessons—these statements appeared:

> The "First Step" is an attempt to separate the mechanical from the *intellectual* in teaching reading—to train the voice even before the philosophy of language is understood...In using the "Exercises" no regard should be paid to the *meaning* of the examples. Let the whole attention be given to articulating the Elementary Sounds and their combinations distinctly and properly and to pronouncing the words correctly (p. 4).

On page 50 of the reader, Tower announced the *next* step in his reading lessons: "Be certain that he [the scholar] fully understands the *meaning* of one extract before he proceeds to another." This step-by-step approach was no doubt easily adaptable to the format of series readers, which during this period gained ascendancy as major instructional tools in American schools.

The step-by-step view of reading differed from the memoriter model in a significant way. It clearly recognized the importance of reading comprehension (intellectual reading) over and above that of rote reading memory while also acknowledging a larger role for silent reading in the acquisition of reading meaning. It likewise recognized the importance of initiating young children into contextual material, but only after they had mastered the mechanical skills required to read the text.

By the 1880s, statements such as the following alluding to the stages or steps in reading appeared in reading series with recurrent frequency:

> The child, prepared to use the *Third Reader*, has passed into the second stage of the work of learning to read. He is able to find ideas in words, and consequently should be required to study and prepare a lesson in reading with comparatively little direct aid from the teacher (*Sheldon's Modern School Third Reader*, c1882, 1883, p. i).

The next step in learning to read is to master the words and forms of expression such as occur in works of accepted standing in literature. Here the difficulty relates to the meaning rather than to the printed form (Harris, c1884, 1885, p. 6).

Contrasting Notions of Reading Comprehension Instruction

Interlocking and step-by-step views of reading implied contrasting notions about reading comprehension instruction. The interlocking view suggested that reading comprehension was facilitated when mechanics and meaning were taught as complementary instructional tasks, whereas the step-by-step view suggested that reading comprehension was facilitated when mechanics and meaning were taught as separate instructional tasks.

The notion of complementary instructional tasks had its initial impact on primary readers. Practices emphasizing comprehension were considered of immediate importance in beginning reading instruction, permitting young children to read *and* react to text as soon as possible. It was believed that these practices also assisted the child's development in the mechanical part of reading, i.e., improved decoding ability, sight vocabulary, and oral reading recitation.

One of the earliest examples of this notion in practice and in print can be found in Gallaudet's *The Mother's Primer* (c1835, 1839) and *The Child's Picture Defining and Reading Book* (c1830, 1833). In Part 1 of his "picture defining" book, a series of seventeen pictures was followed by descriptive phrases that the child was directed to find in the picture by pointing, e.g., "A lively dog." These phrases were followed by sentences that, again, the reader was directed to relate to the elements of the picture, e.g., "The dog is running." Word study, as suggested by Gallaudet in the preface, could be accomplished directly after these activities by using the phrases and sentences in spelling lessons. In Part 2, the same pictures were presented in the same order, followed by a short story about the picture. Gallaudet stated:

> By having attended to these elements which it would be very desirable *briefly to review in each case, before reading the story,* the child is now prepared with the continued aid of the picture to read the story and understand it, with little or no aid from the teacher (p. 3).

A half century after the publication of Gallaudet's book, a teaching procedure using the explanatory mode was suggested in *Harper's Second Reader* (c1883, 1888). It illustrated, in detail, the interweaving of meaning and mechanics in a reading lesson and their mutual reinforcement. Portions of this teaching procedure follow:

Frank and Nellie

1. *Preparation.* What do you see in this picture? Are the children in the country or the city?
2. *Questions to Bring Out the Thought When Oral Reading for the First Time.* How is the first word spelled? Where are Frank and Nellie? Why did they come to the garden? What letter mark is that in the third word of the second paragraph? Read me the third paragraph and tell me what kind of friends Frank and Rover are. What does found mean? What is a telling sentence? Read the sixth paragraph to yourselves. Close your books and tell me what is said in that paragraph.
3. *Review of Lesson.* Tell this story in your own words. Now you may each read the entire lesson (pp. 192-193).

In contrast, the notion of separate instructional tasks dictated the delay of presenting meaningful written text to beginning readers until letters, sounds, and words were mastered. When text was provided, the child's meaningful reaction to the text was either delayed or deemphasized until mechanics were mastered. Mechanical efficiency was required before intellectual mastery could be effected.

Synthetic phonic readers, which became popular in the latter part of the nineteenth century, developed reading lessons based on this notion. Some authors of these programs were convinced that perfect mechanical mastery would automatically result in perfect comprehension of the text. Pollard (1889) wrote the following:

> There must be no guess work (on the part of the child); no reference to pictures; no waiting for a story from the teacher to develop the thought. If instructions in the manual are carefully followed (in inflection, as well as in pronunciation) the child's own voice will give him a perfect understanding of what he reads (pp. 4-5).

These contrasting notions extended upward into the grades, affecting practices there as well. Consider the hypothetical situation of two advanced classes in the 1870s preparing for the reading of Walt Whitman's "Oh Captain, My Captain." In one classroom, the teacher and students discuss their feelings on having lost a loved one, and in the other the teacher is limbering up the voices of students with exercises in elocution dealing with grief and sorrow.

Similar Notions of Reading Comprehension Instruction

Similar notions on the teaching of reading comprehension were implied by the interlocking and step-by-step views on reading. These notions were related to how text requirements and instructional activities (connected to the text) facilitated reading comprehension. One of these notions was a growing awareness of what constituted a comprehensible text: A comprehensible text is not only a decodable text, but a readable text as well. A recent definition of readability indicated that "text and reader variables interact in determining the readability of any given piece of reading material for any given individual reader" (Harris & Hodges, 1981, p. 262).

Although the term *readability* does not appear in the writings of nineteenth century author-educators, there is ample evidence in their readers indicating experimentation in both text and reader variables to improve instruction in intellectual as well as mechanical reading. A major focus of their experimentation was with textual materials for the elementary grades. As early as 1833, Ely wrote:

> Books for little children should be printed on good paper with a fair letter. The lessons should be short and easy on subjects which are familiar to them, and written in language which they can perfectly understand (p. iii).

However, to prepare a comprehensible text for the learner, especially the beginner, was no easy task. Town (1846) expressed this problem as well:

> To combine interest with simplicity, to adopt the style and language to the comprehension of children, and at the same time retain a manly sentiment equally removed from mere childish nonsense on the one hand, and what on the other is altogether above their comprehension, is no easy matter (p. 5).

Authors of more advanced readers likewise were concerned about providing comprehensible text to older students. Hillard (c1856, 1857) wrote in the preface of his *Second Class Reader* that "the aim has been to include no piece that would not be level to the capacity of an intelligent boy or girl of from eleven to thirteen years of age" (p. v).

Kidd (c1870, 1879) included gradation in grammatical complexity in his *Rhetorical Reader for Class Drill and Private Instruction in Elocution*—a feature unique for a student's final book of reading instruction. He wrote:

> The examples (i.e., rhetorical selections) given for practice are so arranged that the student begins with those that are short, simple, readily understood, and easily mastered and is led along progressively to those that are most complex in difficulty (p. iv).

A quarter of a century before Kidd wrote about his grammatical system of gradation, Mandeville (c1846, 1850) already had suggested facilitation of reading comprehension through the emphasis on grammatical teaching and the introduction of reading materials based on grammatical complexity.

Changes in Text Variables and Instructional Practices

Observed changes that occurred in the design of nineteenth century readers to increase their readability are summarized in Table 1. These changes were intended to motivate and capture interest by providing reading materials within the learners' experience and at their level of ability. The text variables cited, however, were put to different uses by different authors to enhance reading comprehension, and selectively used by other authors who did not always agree on the effectiveness of certain text variables to facilitate reading comprehension. One example was the selective use of illustrations and how they contributed to reading comprehension. Different authors intended them for different purposes: to unfold the story (Bentley, c1839, 1857; Butler, 1883); to clarify word meanings (Bentley, c1839, 1857; Besemeres, 1870; Butler, 1883; Gallaudet, c1830, 1833); to enhance sentence meaning (Hillard & Campbell, 1873); and to aid recall (Lovell, c1836, 1852). The varied uses of illustrations increased during the nineteenth century. One publisher noted their importance and their wide public support by entitling an entire reading series *The Illustrated Progressive Series* (c1871, 1876).

There were, however, minority voices that questioned the effectiveness of illustrations in children's readers, agreeing with an earlier nineteenth century view expressed by Hazen (1824): "Pictures in a book were rather an injury than a benefit as they diverted the mind of the child from his lesson, rather than attracted him to it" (p. 4). Ironically, Webb (1855), a staunch supporter of the word method and the explanatory mode, was one such voice that questioned the increased use of pictures in readers to aid comprehension. He believed pictures were "injurious to the child's mind in as much as they dissipate it" (p. v) and, therefore, he kept illustrations at a minimum in his readers.

However, McGuffey's argument on the importance of illustrations in children's texts, cogently stated in his *Eclectic Fourth Reader* (1837), eventually prevailed among author-educators who prepared instructional texts in reading later in the century.

> There is no person but the veriest smatterer [sic] in the business of education, who does not see at once, that visible delineations are indispensable in every grade of education, from primer to the *Principia.* What are maps in Geography, or cuts in Natural History, or diagrams in Geometry, but visible delineations on precisely the same *principle* with pictures and cuts in elementary books for children? (preface)

Another text variable in contention was the practice of vocabulary and/or sentence length control and its effect on reading comprehension. Author-educators who practiced this control called it *gradation,* i.e., a gradual progress in text difficulty within and between readers in the same series. The term *progressive* also was associated with text control, e.g., *The Progressive Fifth or Elocutionary Reader* (Town & Holbrook, c1856) and *The Illustrated Progressive Series* (c1871, 1876). These educators believed that gradation made their readers more decodable and thereby more meaningful to the learner. Those who questioned this practice, or at least its excesses, referred to it as simplification and were seriously concerned about the watering-down of content and the effect this would have on the reader's comprehension. An early, vigorous opponent of simplification was Hall (c1836, 1837), who lamented:

> In attempting and promising to bring everything down to the comprehension of learners it seems to be forgotten that the proper object of education is to elevate the human mind, not to depress it or keep it stationary (p. iv).

The issue of gradation continued to be debated throughout the nineteenth century, with concerns expressed about the use of "mock language" with young readers as well as the tampering of literary pieces for presentation to older students. Some author-educators argued that the text provided in children's readers should be written (1) in a manner that was at least appropriate to the child's own language capacity, and (2) with language and content that expanded the child's mind. Sargent, a vigorous opponent of simplification, presented these arguments in the preface of two of his readers:

Table 1
Text Variables Observed in Readers Designed to Increase Readability*

Text Variable**	Observed Features	Summary
Format The physical appearance of a publication	• Page size • Typeface: size, style • Text signals: typographical devices calling the reader's attention • Margins • Illustrations • Color	In school readers at the elementary level, there was an increase in the size of the page, typeface, and margins, as well as the use of text signals, illustrations, and color.
Typography/Design The process of setting something in type, arranging and printing it	• Number of words per page • Number of sentences per page • Number of unbroken sentences • Number of indentations • Number and arrangement of isolated letters and words on a page	Comparison of children's primary readers published in the early 1800s and later at the turn of the century show a significant decrease in the total number of words and sentences per page, along with an increase in the number of unbroken sentences and paragraph indentations. Also, if letters or words were presented in isolation, there were fewer of them per page.

Table 1 (continued)
Text Variables Observed in Readers Designed to Increase Readability*

Content The subject matter found in a communication source	• Religious • Moralistic • Didactic • Oratorical • Patriotic • Historical • Literary • Informational	The most frequent type of content observed in school readers at the beginning of the nineteenth century was religious, moralistic, didactic, or oratorical in intent and tone. In particular, text instructing children in morals and conduct continued to be favored subject matter for author-educators. By the end of the century, however, readers were emphasizing content dealing with patriotic, historical, literary, and informational materials. Content relating to the child's own interests and experiences likewise increased in frequency over this period (Robinson, 1930).

*The advances in printing technology in the nineteenth century contributed to the development of the comprehensible text.
**Definitions for all text variables except *text control* appear in *A dictionary of reading and related terms,* T. Harris and R. Hodges (Eds.). Newark, DE: International Reading Association, 1981.

Table 1 (continued)
Text Variables Observed in Readers Designed to Increase Readability*

Text Variable**	Observed Features	Summary
Literary Form The how (form) rather than the what (content)	• Prayer • Catechism • Biblical selection • Proverb • Admonition, exhortation • Oration • Dialogue • Letter, journal • Essay, treatise • Descriptive account • Biography/Autobiography • Play • Poem, verse, rhyme • Story	As the nineteenth century progressed, the school reader contained fewer prayers, catechetical exercises, biblical selections, proverbs, admonitions, exhortations, dialogue, and essays. Later nineteenth century readers were more likely to contain descriptive accounts (e.g., historical, scientific), biographical/autobiographical materials, poetry, verse, plays, and stories (Robinson, 1930).

Table 1 (continued)
Text Variables Observed in Readers Designed to Increase Readability*

Text Control The practice of controlling sentence complexity and/or the number and type of words in written text according to specific criteria determined by the author	• Total number of different words introduced in text • Total number of running words in text • Frequency of new words introduced • Frequency that new words are repeated • Limiting new words introduced by predetermined criteria, e.g., number of letters, syllables, phonetic elements, spelling patterns, and/or meaning frequency • Sentence length	This variable had its greatest impact on primary and intermediate grade readers in the latter part of the nineteenth century. Total number of different and running words in a text, length of sentences, and frequency of new words introduced per lesson significantly decreased, whereas the frequency of repeating new words and the practice of limiting them to predetermined criteria increased.

*The advances in printing technology in the nineteenth century contributed to the development of the comprehensible text.

**Definitions for all text variables except *text control* appear in *A dictionary of reading and related terms,* T. Harris and R. Hodges (Eds.). Newark, DE: International Reading Association, 1981.

> It is a narrow experience, I am aware, that would have a pupil read nothing that is not level to his comprehension; that would leave nothing for his mind to grow up to (Sargent, 1863, p. iii).
>
> It has been the author's study while making the reading lessons easy and simple, at the same time to avoid that derogatory style of addressing the young, which many writers seem to regard as one of the conditions of their intelligibility. Their notions of simplicity resemble those of the good lady described in Dickens, who thought she must speak in broken English in order to make herself understood by the poor Italian (Sargent, c1859, 1867, p. iv).

Swinton (c1880, 1882) also was opposed to the excesses of simplification. He believed that his readers had achieved a sensible balance between gradation and challenging material.

> While the greater care has been observed in verbal gradation in this book, it has not been thought necessary to write down to jejuneness. In lessons dealing with concrete subjects that come within the range of the experience of children, or in those easy flights of fancy where the deep interest carries the young reader along with it, words apparently difficult will be found easy of comprehension. In such reading, the pupil is unconsciously led into wider fields of language and becomes by anticipation the reader for the new vocabulary of a higher book (p. iv).

In effect, these authors who identified certain problems resulting from gradation expanded the notion of the comprehensible text to include challenging as well as readable text. Implied in their criticism was that challenging text helped to facilitate reading comprehension if supported by appropriate instructional activities that activated the child's "deep interest, widened experience," and stimulated them through intelligible language that "led into wider fields."

But how were teachers to provide appropriate instructional activities? As early as c1836, Angell recommended "that school books should so be arranged [a reference to text variables] as most effectually to develop and strengthen the mental energies of the pupil" (p. 3), an apparent reference to reading comprehension instruction.

Table 2 summarizes the type of reading comprehension activities that developed during this period to provide the student with such supports. The table identifies (1) the earliest observed date when the activity first appeared or was suggested in the readers examined for this study (dates also are meant to suggest that the types of activities specified were in classroom practice at this time and increased in frequency); (2) the instructional activity as preparatory or follow-up to the reading lesson; (3) the observable text variables authors utilized to support this activity (e.g., printed questions, explanatory notes, illustrations, a suggestion to teachers [STT] appearing in a preface, footnote, or appendix); and (4) the reader (as person) variables these activities intended to activate—the reader's experiential background (E), motivation (M), and/or interest (I).

For example, Table 2 shows that vocabulary study in context was an instructional activity, appearing no later than 1821. It was both preparatory and follow-up to the reading lesson, with intent to activate the learner's experiential background (E). Evidence of this practice appeared in explicit statements made by authors in their prefaces (STT) and can be inferred as well by the specific text variables they used to highlight vocabulary study in context, such as the use of text signals (italicizing, underlining, boldfacing type, placement of words in the margin of texts) to call the reader's attention to a word. It also can be expected that this activity increased in classroom practice after 1821.

It appears from the summary presented in Table 2 that the teacher's role in developing comprehension was substantially expanded when the memoriter model of reading was abandoned by the nineteenth-century educators who became aware that it was not entirely the young scholar's responsibility "to acquire knowledge." These educators contended that the teacher had an active, responsible role in this acquisition other than that of the drillmaster. As expressed by Denman (1851):

> Those who are taught are subject to their teacher's skill; and the book, together with the living teacher, should so instruct the young that the full meaning of every word and sentence,

Table 2
Instructional Activities Recommended to Facilitate Reading Comprehension

Earliest Date Noted	Type of Activity	Text Variable	Reader Variable Activated
	Vocabulary study (preparatory and follow-up)		
1825 (Leonard)	• Word meaning in isolation	• Suggestion to Teachers (STT) • Definitions before or after lesson	E*
c1819 (Adams)	• Word meanings in context	• Text signals such as underlining, italicizing, or boldfacing type, or use of elliptical exercises	
1821 (Perry)	• Dictionary usage	• STT or glossary in appendix	
1826 (Putnam)	• Structural word parts	• Appear before or after lesson, in footnotes, or in a special appendix	
1826 (Putnam)	• Word derivations	• Appear before or after lesson, in footnotes, or in a special appendix	
1807 (Dilworth) 1825 (Cooke) c1833 (Merriam)	• Synonyms, antonyms, homonyms	• Appear before and after lesson, in footnotes, or in a special appendix	

*E = experiential background
M = motivation
I = interest

Table 2 (continued)
Instructional Activities Recommended to Facilitate Reading Comprehension

1822 (Blair) 1824 (Lowe) 1825 (Blake)	Questioning by teacher (preparatory and follow-up)	• STT and/or printed questions in text before or after reading selection or in footnotes	E, M, I
1833 (Emerson)	Discussion related to text (preparatory and follow-up)	• STT	E, M, I
1826 (Putnam) 1826 (Cummings)	Presentation of background information (preparatory)	• STT and/or explanatory notes before or directly after reading selection, in footnotes, or notes in appendix	E
c1830 (Gallaudet)	Use of objects, pictures, or actions to clarify or explain concepts presented in text	• STT and/or illustration appearing in text	E, I

*E = experiential background
M = motivation
I = interest

Table 2 (continued)
Instructional Activities Recommended to Facilitate Reading Comprehension

Earliest Date Noted	Type of Activity	Text Variable	Reader Variable Activated
	Assignments to students for independent work activities		
Prior to 1800	• Vocabulary study (follow-up)	• STT and/or printed assignments appearing in text after reading selection	E, I
1838 (Morley)	• Composition writing		
1835 (Porter) c1846 (Mandeville) 1847 (Weld)	• Language (grammar) study		
c1878 (Raub)	• Research projects		
1883 (Allen)	• Supplementary reading (follow-up)		
1826 (Putnam) 1834 (Worcester)	Study, i.e., silent reading and rereading of text (preparatory)	• STT	E, M, I

*E = experiential background
M = motivation
I = interest

Table 2 (continued)
Instructional Activities Recommended to Facilitate Reading Comprehension

1883 (Butler)	Teacher reading of selection to class followed by discussion (preparatory)	• STT	E, M, I
Prior to 1800	Committing reading selection or parts to memory (preparatory and follow-up)	• STT	E
1833 (Emerson)	Presentation by the teacher of sequence of unified instructional activities designed by the author involving both preparatory and follow-up activities to the reading recitation (preparatory and follow-up)	• STT	E, M, I,

*E =experiential background
M=motivation
I =interest

in all its strength and beauty, would be readily perceived by them (p. v).

Thus, the notion that began to emerge was that appropriate instructional activities, in concert with comprehensible text, could activate the learner to facilitate reading comprehension.

But in what instructional sequence should these activities be presented? If the reading process proceeded in an orderly manner – from the mechanical to the intellectual to the rhetorical – and if the mechanical part of reading proceeded from the alphabet to syllables to words, was there an order of instructional tasks based on a taxonomy of reading that could facilitate reading comprehension? Some nineteenth-century authors apparently believed so, as they searched for the underlying principles upon which reading was based. Sanders (c1859, 1866) wrote that good teaching "assumes that the principles in Reading, as in every other Art, always underlie and regulate the practice" (p. iii). Town (c1847, 1854) was convinced that reading was "a science founded upon principles peculiar to the constitution of man" (p. iii). Tower (c1853, 1860), in his step-by-step *Gradual Readers* discussed earlier, likewise implied the development of reading comprehension based on the orderly presentation of teaching lessons.

By the 1880s, series readers such as *Harper's Second Reader* (c1883, 1888) provided teacher guidelines for directed reading lessons, suggesting a sequence of unified instructional activities that included both preparatory and follow-up lessons to the reading recitation. Although none of the authors of the readers investigated explicitly stated a hierarchy of principles, the notion implied was that there existed a hierarchy of lessons based on underlying principles that when implemented by the teacher facilitated the development of reading comprehension.

The Thought-Getting Model: A View of Reading at the End of the Nineteenth Century (1883-1910)

Ironically, from 1826 to 1882, the rich experimentation by educators to improve reading comprehension was an intermediary objective that had as its final goal excellence in expressive reading. This goal had remained relatively unchanged, although not unchallenged, in American schools since the revolutionary period. Some critics questioned its validity as an instructional goal as early as 1839. For example, Abbot (c1839) wrote in the preface of *The Mount Vernon Reader:* "The end and design of teaching children to read in our schools is not mainly to qualify them for public speaking but for reading either silently to themselves or to a small circle of listeners" (p. 3).

Davis (1839) concurred with this pragmatic observation:

> Perhaps it is not possible for every scholar to attain a high degree of excellence in this department [i.e., rhetorical reading]. There are but few good orators, and but few good musicians; for a similar reason there are but few good rhetorical readers [for] rhetorical excellence is not expected in all readers (p. 48).

These questioning voices, however, were few in a nation that idealized such rhetorical giants as Daniel Webster and Abraham Lincoln. The central role of expressive oral reading in American reading instruction remained steadfast throughout the nineteenth century. As late as 1892, Brown's *Common School Examiner and Review*—a collection of questions used by state, county, and city superintendents in the examination of teachers and pupils—printed a model teacher's examination in reading instruction containing 45 questions related to mechanical and rhetorical reading. Four additional questions pertained to reading comprehension, but none made reference to silent reading instruction.

So strong was the objective of rhetorical excellence in reading education that Clark's *How to Teach Reading in the Public Schools* (c1898, 1899) contained a telling footnote in the introduction: "Throughout this work *reading* is used as an equivalent for oral expression" (p. 8). Clark's footnote may have been defensive for it was made at a time when American educators already had started to challenge the expressive models of reading instruction and were beginning to explore the role of silent reading in reading comprehension instruction.

The Thought-Getting Model of the Reading Process

A revolutionary definition of reading appeared in Parker's *Talks on Teaching* (c1883):

> Reading is getting thought by means of written or printed words arranged in sentences [and] I am sure you have said, as I have given my definition, that reading is the oral expression of thought. That is oral reading. But you will see at once that we may get thought—and by far the greater part of reading is confined to this process—and not give it to others by means of the voice (p. 23).

Parker's definition began with thought-getting and then clearly separated reading into receptive and expressive processes while emphasizing the primacy of silent reading. He asked teachers:

> What is the use of oral reading? Talking enables us to see the child's mind; oral reading to the teacher has no other use. What is the use of [silent] reading? [It] opens to the mind all the learning and erudition of the past...for reading is thinking and thinking is the mind's mode of action (pp. 24-25).

The thought-getting model of the reading process is shown in Figure 4. In this model (1) reading presupposes life experiences; (2) reading is primarily a receptive process (i.e., silent reading) with thought-getting (i.e., thinking) as its goal—a process that involves perceiving text instantaneously (i.e., written or printed words arranged in sentences), associating text with spoken words, and relating these ideas into thought; and (3) reading becomes an expressive act (i.e., oral reading) through thought-giving, when the thought acquired is shared with others.

Parker believed that the driving force of the reading process was the reader's experiential background, and he therefore encouraged teachers to use nontext materials and children's compositions as vehicles to develop reading (Kline, Moore, & Moore, 1987). His perception of the role of life experiences in reading can be gleaned from his instructions to teachers in *Talks on Teaching*, in which he

Figure 4
The Thought-Getting Model (1883-1910)
Reading as a Receptive Process

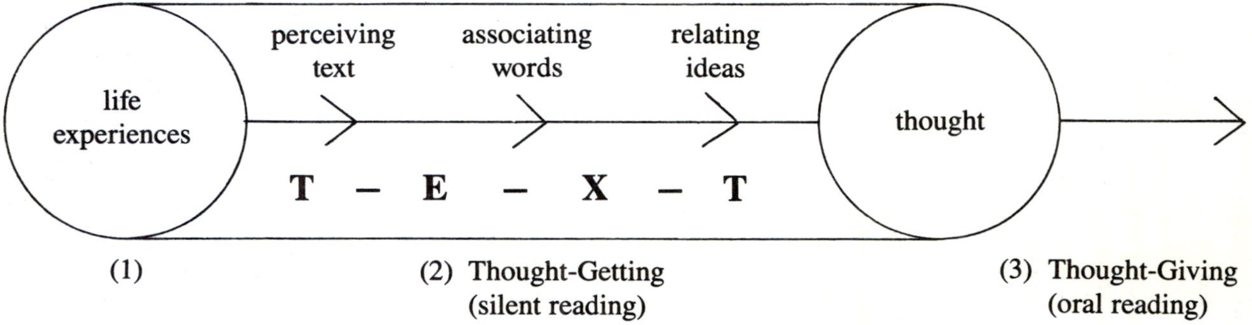

looked upon reading as an associative process. He repeatedly stated in his lectures that "the ideas...associated with spoken words are to be associated with written words [for] this is the sum and substance of learning to read" (p. 24).

Parker's contemporary, Arnold (1894), commenting on the associative aspects of reading, noted the importance of instantaneous perception in the process: "Reading involves knowledge of [a word's] meaning, form and sound, and the perception of the form must instantly suggest the meaning and sound, so close is the association of the three" (p. 154). Arnold also underscored the experiential base required to facilitate the associative process. She observed that "reading pre-supposes living" (p. 160), as was similarly expressed by Farnham (1895), who maintained that "the eye [should] look upon written or printed characters, not as objects to be recognized for their own sake, but as directly calling into conscious being past experiences, and so becoming representative of thought" (p. 14).

Parker's definition of reading also included the requirement of contextual or sentential text. Fragments of words, or isolated words, were excluded from this definition. Since reading was thought-getting, he asserted:

> The word itself should be subordinate and secondary in interest to the child to the idea that excites the mind (p. 31). We do not learn the word in order to read the sentence, but we read the sentence in order to learn the word (p. 32). A thought is ideas in relations and may be called the unit of mental action. A sentence, therefore, is the unit of expression (p. 33).

Farnham (1895) elaborated further on the requirements for sentential text in reading in his teaching manual entitled *The Sentence Method of Reading*. From his experiments with the sentence method, which dated back to 1870 (Reeder, 1900), he stated:

> The first principle to be observed in teaching reading is that things are recognized as wholes. What is the whole? What is the unit of expression? The thought is the unit of thinking [and] it necessarily follows that *the sentence is the unit of*

> *expression*.... A second principle is: We acquire a knowledge of the *parts* of an object by first considering it as a whole.... The sentence being first presented as a whole, the words are discovered, and after that the letters composing the words (p. 17).

On the question of reading as an expressive process, Arnold (1899), who strongly associated reading instruction with our literary heritage, maintained that:

> Nothing is really ours until we have shared it. Our conception of reading is not complete until we have added to our thought-getting, thought-giving (p. 153).

The thought-getting model was a revolutionary perception of reading when compared with its antecedents. In effect, it was a radical development of the interlocking model with which it shared some affinity. It was significantly different in that it gave major roles to experience, silent reading, and thought (i.e., meaning) in the reading process, relegating mechanics and expressive reading to subordinate positions. It also suggested that reading occurred as an inseparable whole rather than in distinct stages for the developing and mature reader, an idea that had tremendous impact on the teaching of reading comprehension.

Interdependent Notions about Reading Comprehension Instruction

The thought-getting view of the reading process was supported by two interdependent notions related to the teaching of reading comprehension.

1. Emphasis on thought-getting throughout the reading activity facilitated reading comprehension. "Let thought lead" became the dictum for this new era in reading (Hervey & Hix, c1911, 1919). Any teaching activity that militated against this goal was to be avoided. For example, Parker, in his lectures to teachers on developing a sight vocabulary, asserted:

> That which aids directly in acts of association of words with their appropriate ideas aids the child in learning to read; any

other method, detail of method or device that does not aid the mind in these acts hinders the child in learning to read (pp. 27-28).

Parker concluded that introducing whole words via the word or object methods in beginning reading was to be preferred to any synthetic approach: "Any attempt to separate the written word into parts or to combine the written parts into a whole, directly and effectually hinders the acts of association and therefore obstructs the action of the child's mind in learning to read" (p. 29).

2. Since thought-getting was a mental (i.e., silent) act requiring "ideas in relation" (i.e., sentential text), it naturally followed that facilitating reading comprehension occurred through the emphasis on silent reading instruction that utilized contextual or sentential text.

Thought-Getting Instructional Practices

The interdependent notions of the thought-getting model profoundly affected reading instruction in the decades following the publication of Parker's lectures, particularly in the primary grades, where the focus of innovative practices occurred. Thought-getting educators strongly agreed with an earlier observation made by Olney (1833) that beginning reading was the crucial period in the child's reading meaning development and the decisive arena in which to solve the problem of reading without thinking.

As the twentieth century was ushered in, so were colorful new readers that made selective use of the four following teaching practices: (1) the sentence and/or story methods, (2) the reading of text silently at the very beginning of reading instruction prior to the oral recitation, (3) the reading lesson unified on the central teaching principle of thought-getting, and (4) decoding through the law of analogies. Descriptions of these reading practices follow.

The sentence and/or story methods. Sentence and story methods incorporated procedures advocated by earlier word and object method educators providing children with meaningful text related to their experience and interest. They were attempts to put into classroom practice the interdependency of all areas of reading instruction. One of the earliest of the new method readers (Allen, Swett, & Royce, c1883, 1899) stated:

> The leading principle in accordance with which this book has been constructed is that, in Primary Reading, the learner should proceed from meaning to form, from idea or thought to the word or sentence expressing it. The *word* and *sentence methods* are in harmony with this idea (p. 3).

Several series readers subsequently appeared with sentence and/or story method exercises that made use of sentential text in the very first pages of the primers. The crucial difference in sentence and story method instruction was in the initial presentation of text.

The story method approach required teachers to tell the story in their own words or to read the complete text to children as it appeared in the reader. The story, often a rhyme or fairy tale with repetitive refrains and predictable outcomes, was to be committed to auditory memory *prior* to the introduction of the written or printed text. "The Little Red Hen" was one such story appearing in several readers. Coe and Christie (c1912) summarized their version of this procedure in the preface of their primer.

> The story is first of all told by the teacher and dramatized by teacher and children together. Thence the work proceeds through the following stages: reading from the blackboard by thought groups; analytic study of thought groups, sentences, word groups, sight words, and phonetics; reading of the whole story aloud from the book (p. 13).

The sentence method took a different tack. The teacher prepared the first reading of the story in piecemeal fashion, introducing through skillful questioning and the use of illustrations one sentence at a time written on the chalkboard or a prepared chart. The sentence was then read by the child. In a sense, children "discovered" their way through the text. Alexander (c1909) stressed the importance of the element of surprise in reading: "Care should be taken...not to spoil the child's surprise in the story found in the book" (p. 118). Arnold (1899) described this practice in the following steps:

1. The sentences of the first lessons should express thoughts in which the children are interested (pp. 66-67).
2. They should be read by the teacher [as the children read along silently] (p. 68).
3. By repetition of these sentences the words are at last held in the mind (pp. 68-69).
4. The [first] words selected for repetition and recognition are...meaningful words (p. 69).
5. When children can recognize...one hundred to two hundred words...likenesses and differences in words are noted...and rules are deduced therefrom (pp. 70-71).

The reading of text silently at the very beginning of reading instruction prior to the oral recitation. Silent reading exercises were stressed by some readers before and/or during the introduction of the child's primer. Preparatory work to the primer generally followed Parker's early suggestions on "chalk talk." He recommended to teachers that "directions be written on the board which the pupil reads silently, and complies with, such as, 'Come to me,' 'Sit down,' or 'Stand up' " (p. 55).

Moore (1909) wrote a 160-page teacher's manual devoted to games that elicited action responses via silent reading from the chalkboard. Action responses were the mainstay activity of silent reading method readers that gained popularity after 1910–almost excluding oral reading as part of the beginning reading instruction. Silent reading method educators not only emphasized the primacy of silent reading, but also were concerned about speed of word perception and developing efficient silent reading rates (Lewis, Rowland, & Gehres, c1924, 1925; Prout, 1928; and Stone & DeWerthern, 1924). Moore (1909) stated:

> The beginning reading matter should be full of action. A child's life is largely made up of action, and his birthright is free motor activity. It is believed that games furnish a better field for the development of child nature. By means of them the power to think quickly, judge, to act as well as to learn politeness, can be unconsciously acquired. It is of the utmost importance that in the beginning of reading advantage be taken of the child's natural impulse to imitate and to play (p. 5).

Silent reading activities printed within the primer text also were used. A claim of the *Werner Primer for Beginners in Reading* (Taylor, c1895), for example, was: "All the sentences in the first lesson direct the performance of some act, thus securing silent reading before oral is attempted" (p. i). Summers' primer (c1908, 1919) also included action response exercises followed by a first reader that made use of printed questions to be read silently but answered orally:

> Where did the lamb go with Mary?
> What would you do if a lamb came to school? (p. 11)

Alexander's primer, *Child Classics* (c1909, 1922), included silent reading exercises such as:

> Give me the answer.
> Do you like John?
> Can you jump the rope?
> Let us _______ Indians.
> Indians _______ run and _____________________ (p. 20).

By combining action responses with object method practices, author-educators at the beginning of the twentieth century were able to introduce silent reading with the initiation of reading instruction.

The reading lesson unified on the central teaching principle of thought-getting. In order to ensure that thought-getting was the overriding goal during reading instruction, sentence and story method readers provided teachers with unified lesson plans for teaching each story in the reader. For example, Summers (1908) made detailed recommendations in the teacher's manual for the presentation of each story, suggesting the following instructional sequence: (1) the development of new words, (2) the silent reading of the complete story, (3) oral reproduction of the complete story (i.e., retelling), and (4) oral reading of the complete story (pp. 7-9, 15-17).

In Burchell's *Plan of Work for the Progressive Road to Reading* (c1909, 1910), a unified teaching plan was recommended.

1. *Oral Work:* Development of Content
   Telling of the story by the teacher
   Conversation on the subject matter of the story
   Oral reproduction of the story by the pupil
2. *Blackboard Work:* Establishing of Relations
   Presentation and formal reading of the first sentence as a whole
   Recognition of words by position in the sentence
   Recognition of words by comparison
   Independent recognition of words
   Drill in rearrangement of words
3. *Book Work:* Reading of the Story as a Whole

Hervey and Hix (c1909, 1923) included the following broad outline for a reading lesson in the teacher's manual:

1. Preparation for the Story
   New words (sight)
   Meaning and use of words
   Thought development: picture study, silent reading, and conversation
2. Oral Reading and Memory Work/Oral Composition
3. Seat Work
4. Spelling
5. Phonics

Decoding through the law of analogies. Thought-getting reading educators required that thinking—not sheer memory—be included during reading lessons that developed word analysis techniques. Their assumption was that *all* reading activities related to thinking developed reading meaning. Thus, they abandoned the drills of the synthetic phonic proponents in favor of a discovery approach that Parker labeled "the law of analogies" and described as follows:

> One of the greatest activities of the mind is the coming together of like to like. It may be called the law of analogies. If the word method were used, pure and simple, the child's unconscious mental activity would seek out and use the

> analogies of the language in associating new written words with the same sounds he has learned to associate with them. When we teach words in phonic order, as, for example, rat, fat, cat, mat, sat, pat, this law of like coming to like in the mind is more effective. But when at the proper time the articulate sounds are consciously associated with the letters that represent them we use the mental activity in the most economical way (pp. 46-47).

As previously noted, Arnold (1899) aptly summarized this procedure for the teacher with this terse statement: "Likenesses and differences in words are noted by the children, and rules are deduced from them" (p. 71). This analytical approach eventually became the phonic way for all story and sentence method readers. As a procedure, it generally followed the introduction of sentential text from which analogous words were selected to generate the rules of phonics.

Counterreaction to the Thought-Getting Model

The ideas propounded by thought-getting proponents had their impact on step-by-step reading educators who were unwilling to entirely abandon the earlier expressive model of reading. Ward (c1894, 1896), author of *The Rational Method in Reading*—a phonic reading series that made extensive use of diacritical markings in its text—made accommodations to the new ideas by designing a first reader that introduced sentential text accompanied by colorful illustrations. Stories in the latter part of his reader, however, were accompanied by diacritical markings for the purpose of extensive phonic training. His diacritical system continued in later readers in his series with minimal emphasis placed on thought-getting.

Fassett (1912) also "endeavored to carry out in [his] phonetic primer the exact principles which Webster embodied in his so-called Spelling Book" (p. iii). However, Fassett's reader was designed for two distinct lines of teaching carried on side by side:

> (1) the drill upon phonetic lists for the purpose of developing phonetic power in the child; and (2) the reading of sim-

> ple stories by the word and sentence method until the child's power in phonetics is far enough advanced to enable him to apply it in his reading lessons (p. v).

In their *New Education Readers* (1900), Demerest and van Sickle claimed to offer "a combination of the best features of the word, phonic, and synthetic methods" (p. 3). Although they upheld intelligent thinking and reading as final goals in instruction, they warned:

> We cannot expect the child to reason for himself during the first year at school. He must have a competent guide and be led to observe, to think and to reason. That guide must of necessity be the teacher, who, in order to attain the highest results must be thoroughly conversant with the method she is to teach (p. 3).

The method they suggested to lead "the child to reason for himself" included these steps:

> The first essential in teaching a child to read is the mastery of words or getting a vocabulary. This is secured through a knowledge of phonics and word building. The next step is the application of that knowledge to the proper construction and intelligent reading of sentences. Intelligent thinking must of necessity precede intelligent reading. This will secure thought reading (p. 4).

The obvious conflicts between expressive and thought-getting models of reading and the differing methods of reading instruction they generated were summarized by Chubb (c1902, 1907) in his teaching methods book:

> Stating the difference between the two...we may say that, for one side, the vital requirement is that a mastery of the mechanism and the acquiring of technical facility should precede the attempt to read in the sense of thought-getting, because the attempt to get thought is hampered by the technical insufficiency; while for the other side, the desire to

> master the thought is regarded as the motive dominating the attempt to master the thought symbols. To one, reading and writing are first indispensable means to and prerequisites of training and culture; to the other they are first steps and integral parts of such training and culture (p. 69).

Chubb's analysis could be applied to the earlier discussion in this chapter of Davis's and Tower's views of reading. Chubb not only described the conflict occurring in American reading instruction at the turn of the century, but also echoed the ongoing concern of educators throughout the nineteenth century regarding the role of thought (i.e., meaning) in the process of teaching reading.

Summary and Concluding Remarks

Views of the reading process and teaching practices in reading comprehension changed during the nineteenth century. Three separate views of the reading process were identified within specified time periods: (1) reading as a facilitator and caretaker of memory (prior to 1826), (2) reading as an expressive art (1826-1882), and (3) reading as a receptive process (1883-1910). From these views, four models of the reading process were inferred, and associated instructional practices were delineated.

1. The memoriter model of reading (prior to 1826) emphasized reading memory over reading comprehension. It supported memoriter–repetitional practices that focused on mastery in decoding, text memorization, study, and oral reading recitation, all intended to preserve reading memory. Automatic decoding was considered the first essential step to reading comprehension.

2. The interlocking model (1826-1882) recognized three interdependent stages in the reading process: mechanical, intellectual, and expressive reading. The model permitted the interweaving of instructional practices in decoding, reading comprehension, and oral reading, recognizing that these activities were mutually supportive.

3. The step-by-step model (1826-1882) recognized three separate stages in the reading process: mechanical, intellectual, and expressive. It supported sequential practices in mechanical and

intellectual reading that were instructionally separated and that required excellence in one stage before the next was attempted. These practices were mainly intended as prerequisites to the final goal of expressive oral reading.

4. The thought-getting model (1883-1910) recognized the importance of experience, silent reading, and thinking in the reading process. It subordinated the roles of decoding and oral reading. The model supported practices that emphasized thought-getting throughout all reading instruction and that required the use of contextual and sentential text and silent reading activities.

Changes in reading comprehension instruction occurred as reading perceptions changed from 1826 to 1910. Overall, the major development in reading comprehension instruction in the nineteenth century was a deemphasis on practices whose goals were memorization of text and rhetorical delivery in favor of practices that activated thought-getting prior to, during, and after silent reading.

The role of mechanical reading as the essential first step of reading comprehension was challenged. Eventually, practices such as decoding and oral reading were accepted by educators as subordinates or complementary adjuncts to the teaching of reading comprehension. Educators began to experiment with innovative practices at all grade levels, but notably at the beginning of reading instruction. Separate practices, such as vocabulary development and teacher questioning, increased in number and frequency to be unified at the turn of the century into sequential lesson plans for teachers. The primacy of silent reading over oral reading gradually became recognized as an instructional activity for school children of all ages and as a life activity for adults. In response to these changes in comprehension practices, school readers were redesigned to increase their readability beyond that of text, emphasizing text variables that appealed to children's needs, interests, and experiences.

The close of this period (around 1910) found thought-getting and silent reading practices in ascendancy in American schools, with intimations that a future methodology in reading would be based on the learner's inner experiences and expression. This time also heralded the new science of educational research, with its focus on the assumptions and hypotheses that were expounded and put into practice by author-educators in their readers during the nineteenth century.

References

Abbott, J. *The Mount Vernon reader.* Boston, MA: W. Crosby, c1839, 1840.

Adams, D. *The understanding reader.* Leicester, MA: Hori Brown, c1819, 1821.

Alden, A. *The reader: An easy and systematical method of teaching and of learning the English language,* fifth edition. Boston, MA: James Loring, c1802, 1822.

Alexander, G. *Child classics.* Indianapolis IN: Bobbs-Merrill, c1909, 1922.

Allen, C.H. *Indiana state series: Second reader.* Indianapolis, IN: State of Indiana, 1883.

Allen, C.H., Swett, J., and Royce J. *First reader.* Indianapolis, IN: Indiana School Book, c1883, 1899.

Angell, O. *The select reader.* Philadelphia, PA: W. Marshall, c1836, 1838.

Arnold, S.L. *Reading: How to teach it.* Boston, MA: Silver, Burdett, 1899.

Arnold, S.L. *Waymarks for teachers, showing aims, principles, and plans of every day teaching with illustrative lessons.* New York: Silver, Burdett, 1894.

Barbauld, A.L.A. *The female speaker: Miscellaneous pieces of prose and verse, selected from the best writers, and adapted to the use of young women.* Boston, MA: Wells & Lilly, 1824.

Bentley, R. *The pictorial spelling book: Containing an improved method of teaching the alphabet.* New York: Farmer, Brace, c1839, 1857.

Benton, N.S. *Statutes of the state of New York relating to common schools,* including title ii of chapter xv. Part i of the revised statutes as amended by the act chapter 480, laws of 1847 with forms and regulations respecting proceedings under those statutes. Albany, NY: C. Van Benthuysen, Public Printer, 1847.

Besemeres, J. *Picture teaching for young and old.* London: Cassell, Petter, & Galpin, 1870.

Bingham, C. *The Columbian orator, containing a variety of original and selected pieces, together with rules calculated to improve youth and others in the ornamental and useful art of eloquence,* sixth edition. Troy, NY: Parker & Bliss, 1815.

Blair, H. *Pictures on rhetoric.* Brookfield, MA: E. Merriam, 1822.

Blake, J.L. *The historical reader.* Concord, NH: Isaac Hill, 1825.

Brown, I.H. *Common school examiner and review,* revised edition. Chicago, IL: Flanagan, 1892.

Bumstead, J.F. *My first school-book, to teach me to read and spell words, and understand them.* Boston, MA: T.R. Marvin, c1852, 1859.

Burchell, G., Ettinger, W.L., Shimer, E.D., and Peyser, N. *Plan of work for the new progressive road to reading.* New York: Silver, Burdett, c1909, 1910.

Butler, E.H. *Butler's series: The second reader.* Philadelphia, PA: E.H. Butler, 1883.

Carter, J.G. (Ed.). Interrogatory instruction. *American Journal of Education,* 1829a, *4,* 142-157.

Carter, J.E. (Ed.). Thoughts on primary education: Elementary instruction in the English language. *American Journal of Education,* January/December 1829b, *4,* 385-394.

Chubb, P. *The teaching of English in the elementary and secondary schools.* New York: Macmillan, c1902, 1907.

Clark, S.H. *How to teach reading in the public schools.* Chicago, IL: Scott, Foresman, c1898, 1899.

Cobb, L. *Cobb's juvenile reader, number 3.* New York: Collins & Hannay, c1831, 1833.

Cobb, L. *Cobb's spelling book,* revised edition. Ithaca, NY: Mack & Andrus, c1825, 1831.

Coe, I., and Christie, A.D. *Story hour readers, primer,* revised edition. New York: American Book, c1912, 1923.

Cooke, A.J. *The student's companion,* second edition. Concord, NH: Isaac Hill, 1825.
Cooke, I. *The American orator; or elegant extracts in prose and poetry: Comprehending a diversity of oratorical specimens, of the eloquence of popular assemblies, of the bar, of the pulpit, etc.* Hartford CT: Oliver D. Cooke, 1814.
Crosby, W.E. *Our little book for little folks.* New York: American Book, 1896.
Cummings, J.A. *The pronouncing spelling book.* Bellows Falls, VT: James I. Cutter, 1826.
Davis, E. *The teacher taught; or, the principles and modes of teaching.* Boston, MA: Marsh, Capen, Lyon, & Webb, 1839.
Demerest, A.J., and van Sickle, W.M. *New education readers: Book one.* New York: American Book, 1900.
Denman, J.S. *Third reading book.* New York: Pratt, Woodforce, 1851.
Diack, H. *In spite of the alphabet.* London: Chatto & Winders, 1965.
Dickinson, R. *The Columbian reader.* Boston, MA: R.P. & C. Williams, 1821.
Dilworth, T. *A new guide to the English tongue* (in five parts). Glasgow, Scotland: Printed by Niven, Napier & Khull for A. Wilson, and Gardner & Hutchinson, 1807.
Ely, J. *The child's instructer [sic]: Consisting of easy lessons for children on subjects which are familiar to them in language adapted to their capacities by a teacher of little children in Philadelphia.* Bridgeport, CT: J.B. & L. Baldwin, 1833.
Emerson, B.D. *The first-class reader.* Philadelphia, PA: Hogan & Thompson, c1833, 1836.
Farnham, G.L. *The sentence method of reading.* Syracuse, NY: C.W. Bardeen, 1895.
Fassett, J.H. *The Beacon primer.* Boston: Ginn, 1912.
Gallaudet, T.H. *The child's picture defining and reading book,* third edition. Hartford, CT: F.J. Huntington, c1830, 1833.
Gallaudet, T.H. *The mother's primer,* fifth edition. Hartford, CT: Spalding & Storrs, c1835, 1839.
Guthrie, J.T. (Ed.) *Reading: William S. Gray. A research retrospective, 1881-1941.* Newark, DE: International Reading Association, 1984.
Hall, J. *The reader's guide.* Hartford, CT: Canfield & Robins, c1836, 1837.
Hall, S.R. *Lectures on school reading.* Boston, MA: Richardson, Lord & Hollbrook, 1829.
Harper's second reader. New York: American Book, c1883, 1888.
Harris, T.L., and Hodges, R.E. (Eds.). *A dictionary of reading and related terms.* Newark, DE: International Reading Association, 1981.
Harris, W.T. *Appleton's school readers: Introductory fourth reader.* New York: Appleton, c1884, 1885.
Hazen, J. *The primary instructor and improved spelling book.* Woodstock, VT: D. Watson, 1824.
Hervey, W.L., and Hix, M. *The Horace Mann readers: Fourth reader.* New York: Longman, Green, c1911, 1919.
Hervey, W.L. and Hix M. *The Horace Mann readers: Teacher's manual, third reader.* New York: Longman, Green, c1909, 1923.
Hillard, G.S. *Second class reader.* Boston, MA: Hickling, Swan, & Brown, c1856, 1857.
Hillard, G.S., and Campbell, L.J. *The Franklin primer or first reader.* New York: Taintor Brothers, Merrill. Boston, MA: W. Ware, 1873.
The illustrated progressive series. New York: P. O'Shea, c1871, 1876.
Johnson, C. *Old-time schools and school books.* New York: Macmillan, c1904, 1917.
Keagy, J.M. Early intellectual education. *American Journal of Education,* 1826, *1,* 672-680.
Kidd, R. *A rhetorical reader for class drill and private instruction in elocution.* Cincinnati, OH: Wilson, Hinkle, c1870, 1879.
Kirk, M. *The Baldwin primer.* New York: American Book, 1899.
Kline, E., Moore, D.W., and Moore, S.A. Colonel Francis Parker and beginning reading instruction. *Reading Research and Instruction,* 1987, *26* (3), 141-150.
Knell, A. *The phonic reader for common schools,* number one. Cincinnati, OH: Wilson, Hinkle, c1868.

Knudson, C.W. *A primer for use in schools and families for teaching correct and distinct articulation in reading and speaking.* South Norwalk, CT: Golden Bros., c1887.
Leavitt, J. *Reading lessons for the use of the middle classes in common schools.* Boston, MA: John P. Jewett, c1847, 1852.
Leonard, L.W. *The literary and scientific class books.* Keene, NH: John Prentiss, c1825, 1827.
Lewis, W.D., Rowland, A.L., and Gehris, E.H.M. *The silent readers' manual.* Philadelphia, PA: J.C. Winston, c1924, 1925.
Longley E. *Furst fonetic redur.* Boston, MA: Otis Clapp, 1852.
Lovell, J.E. *The young pupil's second book.* New Haven, CT: S. Babcock, c1836, 1852.
Lowe, A.T. *The Columbia class book,* second edition. Worcester. MA: Doir & Howland, c1824, 1825.
Mandeville, H. *A course of reading for common schools and the lower classes of academies.* New York: D. Appleton, c1846, 1850.
Marrou, H.I. *A history of education in antiquity.* George Lamb, translator. Madison, WI: University of Wisconsin Press, 1982. This is a translation of *Histoire de l'éducation dans l'Antiquité,* third edition. Paris: Seuil, 1948.
Mathews, M.M. *Teaching to reading, historically considered.* Chicago, IL: University of Chicago Press, 1966.
McGuffey, W.H. *Eclectic first reader.* Cincinnati, OH: Truman & Smith, 1836.
McGuffey, W.H. *Eclectic fourth reader.* Cincinnati, OH: Truman & Smith, 1837.
Merriam, G. *The American reader,* second edition. Brookfield, MA: George Merriam, 1829.
Merriam, G. *The child's guide comprising familiar lessons designed to aid in correct reading, spelling, defining, thinking, and acting.* Springfield, MA: George Merriam, c1833, 1847.
Moore, M. *Blackboard reading.* Boston, MA: Educational Publishing, 1909.
Morley, C.A.B. *A practical guide to compositon.* Hartford, CT: R. White, c1838, 1839.
Olney, J. *The easy reader; or, introduction to the national preceptor.* New Haven, CT: Durrie & Peck, 1833, 1839.
Parker, F.W. *Talks on teaching.* New York: Barnes, c1883.
Perkinson, H.J. Introduction: American textbooks and educational change. In D. Svobodny (Ed.), *Early American textbooks.* Washington, DC: U.S. Department of Education, 1985, ix-xv.
Perry, W. *The only sure guide to the English tongue or Perry's spelling book,* sixth edition. Brookfield, MA: E. Merriam, c1821, 1823.
Pierpont, J. *The young reader: To go with the spelling book.* Boston, MA: Carter, Hendee, c1830, 1833.
Pollard, R. *Pollard's synthetic method of reading and spelling.* New York: American Book, 1889.
Porter, E. *The rhetorical reader.* New York: Mark Newman, c1835, 1849.
Prout, F.J. *Thought test readers, primer.* Lincoln, NH: University Publishing, 1928.
Putnam, S. *The analytical reader.* Portland, ME: William Hyde, c1826, 1836.
Putnam, S. *The reader and speaker.* New York: French & Alard, 1836.
Raub, A.N. *The new normal reader.* Chicago, IL: Werner, c1878, 1894.
Reeder, R.R. *The historical development of school readers and of methods in teaching reading.* New York: Macmillan, 1900. Also in Columbia University *Contributions to Philosophy, Psychology, and Education,* 1900, *8* (2).
Robinson, R.R. *Two centuries of change in the content of school readers.* Nashville, TN: George Peabody College for Teachers (press of William's Printing), 1930.
Sanders, C.W. *Sanders school readers, fifth book.* New York: Ivison, Phinney, & Blakeman, c1859, 1866.
Sanders, C.W. *Sanders' union fifth reader.* New York: Ivison, Blakeman, & Taylor, c1867, 1878.

Sanders, C.W. *Sanders' union pictorial primer.* New York: American Book Company, c1866, 1893.
Sargent, E. *The standard first reader: Part two.* Boston, MA: J.L. Shorey, c1860, 1866.
Sargent, E. *The standard third reader: Part two, with spelling and defining lessons.* Boston, MA: J.L. Shorey, 1863.
Sargent, E. *The standard fifth reader, or first class reader.* Boston, MA: J.L. Shorey, 1863.
Sheldon & Co's. modern school first reader. New York: Sheldon, c1881, 1883.
Sheldon & Co's. modern school third reader. New York: Sheldon, c1882, 1883.
Smith, N.B. *American reading instruction.* Newark, DE: International Reading Association, 1965, 1986.
Staniford, D. *The art of reading.* Boston, MA: West & Richardson, c1815, 1817.
Stone, C.R., and De Werthern, H. *Stone's silent reading, book one.* Boston, MA: Houghton Mifflin, 1924.
Strong, T. *The common reader.* Greenfield, MA: Denio, Clark & Tyler, 1824.
Strong, T. *The young scholar's manual.* Greenfield, MA: Denio & Phelps, c1819, 1822.
Summers, M. *The Summers' readers manual.* New York: L.A. Noble, 1908.
Summers, M. *The Summers' readers: Primer and first reader.* New York: L.A. Noble, c1908, 1919.
Swan, W.D. *The primary school reader.* Philadelphia, PA: Thomas Cowperthwait, c1844, 1847.
Swinton, W. *Swinton's supplementary readers.* New York: Ivison, Blakeman, & Taylor, c1880, 1882.
Swinton, W. *Swinton's third reader.* New York: Ivison, Blakeman, & Taylor, 1882.
Taylor, F.L.D. *The Werner primer for beginners in reading.* Chicago, IL: Werner School, c1895.
Tower, D.B. *The gradual primer or primary school enunciator, part one.* New York: Cady & Burgess, c1845, 1852.
Tower, D.B. *The gradual reader: The child's first step taken in the right place.* Boston, MA: Sanborn, Carter, & Bazin, c1853.
Tower, D.B. *The gradual reader: First step of exercises in articulation.* Boston, MA: Sanborn, Carter & Bazin, c1853, 1860.
Town, S. *The child's first book.* Cooperstown. NY: H. & E. Phinney, c1845, 1846.
Town, S. *The fourth reader.* Portland, ME: Blake & Carter, c1847, 1854.
Town, S., and Holbrook, N.M. *The progressive fifth or elocutionary reader.* Boston, MA: O. Ellsworth, c1856.
Town, S. and Holbrook, N.M. *The progressive fourth reader.* Boston, MA: Bazin & Ellsworth, 1857.
The Tract Primer. New York: American Tract Society, c1848. (Frances Manwaring Caulkins, 1795-1869, is credited with authorship.)
Tuer, A.W. *History of the Hornbook,* volumes one and two. Amsterdam, The Netherlands: S. Emmering, 1971. (Unchanged reprint of the original edition published in London, 1896.)
Venezky, R.L. A history of the American textbook. *Elementary School Journal,* 1987, *87* 247-265.
Ward, E.G. *The rational method in reading.* New York: Silver, Burdett, c1894, 1896.
Webb, J.R. *Normal reader; number 1.* New York: Sheldon, Lamport, & Blakeman, 1855.
Webb, J.R. *Normal reader; number 4.* New York: G. Savage & Mason & Law, c1850, 1853.
Webster, N. *A grammatical institute of the English language, Part one.* Hartford, CT: Hudson & Goodwin, 1783.
Webster, N. *An American dictionary of the English language.* New York: S. Converse, 1828.
Weld, A.H. *Parsing book.* Portland, ME: O.L. Sanborn, 1847.
Westerhoff. J.H. III, *McGuffey and his readers.* Nashville, TN: Abingdon, 1978.
Wickersham, J.P. *Methods of instruction.* Philadelphia: J.B. Lippincott, c1865.

Willard, S. *The general class book, or interesting lessons in prose and prose and verse, on a great variety of subjects combined with an epitome of English orthography and pronunciation, and intended as the third book in a course of reading for the use of schools.* Greenfield, MA: A. Phelps and A. Clark, 1828.

Worcester, S. *A fourth book of lessons for reading.* Boston, MA: C.J. Hendee and Jenks & Palmer, c1834, 1845.

Wooster, L.E. *The Wooster primer.* Topeka, KS: Crane, 1899.

3

Reading Comprehension Instruction in America: 1910-1987

In Chapter 2, inferences about the teaching of reading comprehension were drawn from authoritative opinion and instructional materials. With the advent of research related to reading instruction during the second decade of the twentieth century, it became possible to view the actual research focused on reading comprehension instruction—the major goal of this monograph. The first few pages of this chapter consist of an introduction to the historical background of the research on teaching or improving reading comprehension instruction and a brief discussion of research designs and emphases. The bulk of the chapter consists of a discussion of 11 categories of methods used in the teaching of reading comprehension across the years:

- exercises and drills,
- teacher-directed skill lessons,
- rereading,
- reading practice,
- study skills,
- instrument presentations,
- word study,
- oral presentations,
- schema activation,
- text structure, and
- monitoring.

Method of Study

Sources

Three hundred sixty-nine studies were selected from the following sources: the *Annual Summaries of Investigations Relating to Reading,* edited by Sam Weintraub and others (IRA); research reports printed on microfiche in the William S. Gray Research Collection in Reading (Alvina Treut Burrows Institute, Manhasset, New York); and early *Yearbooks* of the National Society for the Study of Education (NSSE). The survey of over 18,000 research reports resulted in the 369 studies (about 2 percent of all the published research in reading) that were focused on reading comprehension instruction.

Many researchers dealt with reading comprehension in one way or another, but relatively few conducted studies of instruction in reading comprehension. Our criteria for the selection of research reports were the intent of the investigator to provide instruction in reading comprehension and sufficient information in the report to delineate the nature of the instruction.

We did not include studies just because a reading comprehension measure was used as a pre and/or posttest. We included studies only when we believed that the researchers' major purpose was to improve or teach reading comprehension. For example, we included a study that was part of the First Grade Cooperative Research reports (Bond & Dykstra, 1967) only when an individual researcher set out to specifically teach reading comprehension.

When investigators indicated that they set up a program aimed at teaching or improving reading comprehension, but gave no indication of the nature of the program, their investigations were not included in this monograph. Studies that were included ranged from those in which the names of materials or skills/strategies were merely mentioned to those that contained explicit information.

Procedure

When the review process was started several years ago, the *Annual Summaries* provided initial information that took us to the full reports on microfiche in the Gray Collection. Although methodology studies were classified in the *Annual Summaries,* a group of doctoral students read through summaries of the total number of reading studies in the Gray Collection, regardless of classification, to be certain no study was missed. The most recent, pertinent investigations not yet published in the Gray Collection at the time this monograph was written were located in libraries. The early *Yearbooks* on reading published by NSSE were consulted for historical background on research in the teaching of reading comprehension. The 11 categories of methods of teaching reading comprehension discussed in this chapter emerged from our review of the literature.

Historical Background

Before 1910

Prior to 1884 there were no research reports (published in English) focused on reading. From 1884-1910 there were only 35 published studies, and they were primarily laboratory investigations unrelated to pedagogy; hence, they were not included in the period covered in Chapter 2. There was, however, 1 study published prior to 1910 that was a precursor for a number of future investigations, although it was not focused on instruction. This first piece of research related to reading was conducted by Romanes (1884) and reported in his book, *Mental Evolution in Animals.* As a result of his study of the reading of adults, he concluded that material must be read twice in order to be fully understood. Although this first reading researcher was not consciously concerned with the teaching of reading comprehension, he stumbled upon a baseline assumption to be tested by a number of subsequent investigators.

As shown in Chapter 2, a limited number of pre-1910 researchers and theorists called attention to the distinctions between oral and silent reading and, in doing so, were harbingers of things to come. Silent reading soon unseated oral reading as the emphasis of reading instruction and the focal point for studies concerned with reading comprehension.

The "scientific movement" in education was ushered in with Thorndike's handwriting scale published in 1910, followed by Gray's standardized oral reading paragraphs in 1915. A host of standardized silent reading tests were published in the ensuing years. During this time period a large percentage of the investigations focused on the standardization and application of reading tests. However, a substantial number of researchers were concerned with learning more about silent reading, for with the advent of World War I, the country learned that "thousands of our soldiers could not read well enough to follow printed instructions used in connection with military life" (Smith, 1986, p. 158).

Gray (1917) was an instrumental force in promoting silent reading as a powerful means of improving reading comprehension. Based on a review of the existing research, he made several suggestions related to reading comprehension instruction that guided research directions not only during this period but even today: (1) A student's prior knowledge that he/she will be responsible for understanding the material improves the quality of reading. (2) Emphasis on those elements upon which meaning depends improves comprehension. (Among these elements, Gray cited topic sentences, relational words, types of modifying phrases, and, interestingly enough, the requiring of written reproduction—a requirement not seriously heeded across the years unless filling in blanks and writing brief responses are thought of as written reproduction.) (3) Fast readers are usually better comprehenders than slow readers. Gray indicated, however, that research demonstrated that pushing students to read too fast harmed comprehension. In the studies on reading comprehension improvement explored in the preparation of this monograph, there was little evidence that comprehension suffered with rate improvement. It did seem true that, after instruction, rates of reading were subject to more immediate and dramatic improvement than was comprehension.

In 1925 a National Committee on Reading was appointed by the Commissioner of the Bureau of Education and, as reflected in its report (Whipple, 1925), emphasis was placed on "intelligent" reading (comprehending and interpreting) as a reaction to the earlier notions of reading as a direction for the future. However, in *The Measurement of Understanding* (Henry, 1946), Douglass and Spitzer bemoaned the fact that:

> Traditionally, teaching methods have neglected or minimized understandings as learning outcomes. Instead, they were designed primarily to develop the ability to recite words or to perform skills in response to the specific cues of classroom questions and commands. The learning which took place was slight in amount; too often it was superficial and artificial; and it was relatively useless. It could be applied neither to other segments or units of knowledge nor to life needs, and it was soon forgotten....Reading was not viewed as a thought-getting process. Rather, the aim seemed to be the development of mechanical proficiency in the recognition of the printed word, and it was assumed that this proficiency would operate satisfactorily however and whenever reading was engaged in. As a consequence, too few children acquired the techniques (or even realized the necessity) of understanding what they read, together with its meaning, its significance, and its potential applications to life experiences (pp. 8-10).

In 1949, for the first time, an entire chapter in an NSSE *Yearbook* was devoted to comprehension (Durrell, 1949). The chapter was entitled "Development of Comprehension and Interpretation." Durrell reported two general approaches to the improvement of comprehension evident in school programs: (1) "The related activity approach which recognizes that meaning rests upon experience and that the ultimate use of reading is in enriching the activities of life"; and (2) "the reading-skills approach which gives the child systematic practice in the basic skills needed for effective reading." He suggested that "a balanced program in reading comprehension will utilize both approaches and will adapt them to individual and group needs" (p. 194).

In an earlier NSSE *Yearbook* (Whipple, 1937), Gray stated that "great improvement has been made in methods of teaching reading, resulting in increased emphasis upon the meaning or content of what is read and in the elimination of much of the formal drill required in the past" (p. 8). Unfortunately, neither Durrell's nor Gray's observations were evident in the research literature related to reading comprehension instruction of that period. Most of the studies reflected the teaching of subskills through drill. An assumption, also visible in the studies of today, appeared to be the notion that once the skills were named and/or described by the teacher or by written material, drill would result in improvement and transfer. Little direct teaching was evident, at least in the reports as written.

From 1910 to 1950, studies often were undertaken because students had obtained poor scores on standardized reading tests. In addition, during the 1940s, efforts were made to help adults, as once again war made the country aware of the need to improve reading instruction at all levels. Until recently, few investigators looked at the process of comprehending as contrasted to the product of reading comprehension. Through the years, a substantial number used prereading activities or preorganizers as a means of improving reading comprehension, but goals were frequently narrow and temporal. In a survey of 119 articles on what research revealed about teaching practices in reading, McCullough (1957) observed:

> Throughout many of the studies consulted there runs the thread that we get what we work for consciously; that if both students and teacher are aware of the specific goals, those specific goals are more apt to be reached. Along with this finding, however, runs the danger that narrowly conceived goals produce limited results. We must work for specific goals consciously, but those specific goals need to encompass a broad definition of reading skills if the product is not to be dwarfed and distorted (p. 475).

During the same year as McCullough's review and comments, the launching of Sputnik threw education into the task of upgrading its traditional curricula. In 1965 Congress passed the Elementary and Secondary Education Act, which designated the largest sum of money ever appropriated for education—up to that time—with a healthy portion of the funds assigned to reading instruction and reading research. From 1965 to the present, that Act has been influential in promoting instructional innovations and research designs, despite its funding "ups and downs." This fresh interest in research, coupled with multiple perspectives from related disciplines, spawned a number of models that defined reading as a unitary process of seeking meaning from print rather than as an accumulation or hierarchy of skills. The development of models and theories based on concepts from a number of other disciplines – linguistics, psycholinguistics, sociolinguistics, information processing, cognitive psychology, anthropology, and sociology – led to the testing of strategies based on text structure, the background knowledge of the reader, and the context of the reading act.

The limited number of studies done most recently do seem to be moving in the direction of procedures linked to larger units of text through such procedures as questioning, outlining, and summary writing rather than the prior emphasis on the development of subskills through workbooks, worksheets, and other types of exercises. Feedback allowing for the development of self-monitoring has only just begun to receive emphasis.

Most investigators who focused on the teaching of reading comprehension rarely attempted to teach the transfer of what they taught to other situations. They undoubtedly wanted transfer to take place, but they did not design their studies to assess that dimension. Several of the early researchers wrote of transfer as successful scores on standardized reading tests of reading comprehension following their drills on skills similar to those on the tests. Today, transfer to novel materials and to other situations and contexts is emphasized in theory and philosophy. At the time of this writing, however, few researchers have designed studies to incorporate adequate transfer of the successful application of a reading comprehension strategy taught in one context to diverse situations.

Research Methodology

Between 1910 and 1925, most investigators concerned with the teaching of reading comprehension did not make use of the emerging statistical concepts evident in other disciplines; findings were usually reported by comparing scores, often in percentages. Many provided hazy descriptions of subjects, procedures, and findings. Most of the studies in which there was an attempt to control a few variables were, as today, quasi experimental. A large number fell into the category of action research in which educators were attempting to improve reading instruction through the introduction of new programs or skills with no further control than pre and posttesting.

From the late 1920s through the late 1940s, designs still tended to be rather unsophisticated, even for that time, although tests of significance were used frequently. A problem emerged (still evident in the research of today) of using investigator-designed instruments without ascertaining validity or reliability; conclusions and implications for instruction frequently were based on the results of informal, untested instruments.

In the 1950s and 1960s, there was a movement away from the assessment of performance by standardized reading tests and informal multiple-choice tests toward the use of free recall and protocol analysis. A remaining hurdle is to convince some school personnel and political leaders that scores on standardized tests are not the sole way of evaluating literacy.

From the 1970s on, researchers did turn to more complex designs and statistical procedures. There was frequent use of analyses of variance and covariance. There was more concern for multiple comparisons: levels of ability, sex, subtle changes in treatments, and variations in learning conditions. Although the advent of the computer and more sophisticated statistical tools appeared to increase research productivity, dissatisfaction in the early 1980s with the lack of fresh insights gained from sophisticated experimental designs appeared to spark the growth and the acceptance of naturalistic, ethnographic, field-based studies.

Whatever the research design, an unfortunate aspect of research reports over the years is that most have been published in journals with page constraints. Hence, too frequently, journals do not contain enough detailed information to permit replication.

Finally, especially in the years prior to the 1970s and 1980s, investigators often did not provide careful reviews and analyses of prior research and theory in their reports. It was infrequent to find a comprehensive and critical review of the literature. Similarly, some present day researchers who do review the literature appear not to have read anything earlier than the start of ERIC in 1966.

Inferred Methods for Teaching Reading Comprehension

The 11 categories of methods delineated and discussed in this chapter are based on the 369 individual studies that focused on reading comprehension instruction from 1918 through June 1987. Some of the studies have been referred to only as examples to elucidate the discussion. An overview of all of the studies may be found in Appendix A, along with an alphabetical listing of the studies in Appendix B.

The order of the categories of methods is not precisely chronological, although there is a general, but overlapping, historical progression from those discussed first to those discussed last. The reader must bear in mind throughout the ensuing discussion that some of the methods categorized here may not be considered teaching methods today. These methods relate back to the 27 inferred definitions listed in Chapter 1 (this book). This is a historical view of methodology in which the authors have attempted to ascertain what the researchers of the time considered to be methodology for teaching reading comprehension.

Exercises and Drills

As shown in Chapter 2, from the second half of the nineteenth century through the beginning of the twentieth, some educators advocated the teaching of silent reading, advancing the arguments that most people had little occasion to read aloud and most reading tasks were silent. At the same time these voices began to be heard and instruction started to turn in that direction (during the early 1900s), the scientific movement in education burst upon the scene. Standardized tests of silent reading began to be used in schools. The comprehension parts of these tests usually called for the reader to select main ideas and details in a multiple-choice format for isolated paragraphs of texts. Occasionally, readers also were asked to choose inferences and conclusions. Teachers, unaccustomed to teaching silent reading, found their students floundering on the tests. Remedial reading was born overnight, and the seemingly logical introduction of exercises and drills related to the skills assessed on the tests, as well as the reading of directions, became highlighted as a means of teaching reading comprehension. As a justification for her study in which primary subjects were drilled on skills, Slama (1923) stated:

> Silent reading in the lower grades is now the most important problem confronting the primary teacher. Heretofore, the main problem of the teacher was the teaching of oral reading; but no, oral reading has been slated as an elocutionary art and not as a factor greatly needed by the child. The greatest part of a child's life is spent in reading to learn, and not in learning to read (p. 142).

Over 20 percent of all the studies concerned with teaching reading comprehension fell into this category of exercises and drills, two-thirds of them published in the 1920s and 1930s. A brief resurgence occurred during the 1960s with the publication of kits and programmed materials.

The terms *exercises* and *drills* often were used interchangeably. In general, they aimed to improve a skill or group of skills through a series of similar materials, commercial or teacher prepared, worked on independently or semi-independently by students at all grade levels. In the early years, the concentration most often was on the reading of paragraphs and finding main ideas and subordinate details, as well as the reading of directions—the skills most frequently found on standardized tests of silent reading.

From the 1920s through the 1930s, the most popular commercial exercises (at least of those reported in the studies surveyed in the preparation of this monograph) were the McCall-Crabbs Test Lessons in Reading (still used by Maddison & Rimmington in 1966). Those researchers who developed their own exercises created materials ranging from skillsheets to units involving large pieces of text. The few "exercise" studies published in the 1970s were directed more toward factors such as the use of logical inference rules (Lowerre & Scandura, 1974) or sentence expansion (Froese & Kurushima, 1979).

Between 1920 and 1924 with elementary subjects, in 1931 with high school students, and in 1934 with college students, researchers drilled on the actual standardized test items and/or repeatedly administered different forms of standardized tests as a way of improving reading comprehension. Gates and Van Alstyne (1924) suggested that such drill and repetition made students more testwise and, hence, increased their scores, but they were uncertain whether reading comprehension was really improved. In 1926, both Alderman and Miles, in separate studies, raised questions about the value of drill. They commented that better students lost interest and showed no marked improvement. Little or no attention was paid to the critics for many years.

Teacher-Directed Skill Lessons

The concept of direct teaching was hard to pin down for lack of clarity in the research reports; it is conceivable that more teacher-directed instruction was conducted in the studies reported in the exercise category, but haziness of reporting made it unclear whether any direct teaching took place. However, about 5 percent of all studies scattered throughout the period (mainly in grades three to eight) focused on more than just attempts to supervise the practice of skills. This group of investigators frequently helped students work with larger pieces of text, stressing superordinate-subordinate ideas. It is in this category that we see the use of the DRA, the DRTA, the ReQuest technique, and lessons in and applied to content areas. For example, Dearborn and Wilking (1941) focused on the thorough reading of selections, organizational patterns, and associative reading—"the reader's participation in what the writer is attempting to express" (p. 672). Others (as recently as Taylor, 1986, who devised a strategy for teaching main ideas to middle graders) concentrated on a given skill.

What is meant by such direct teaching often has been hazy across the years of studies. Either journal space delimited detailed descriptions of how something was taught, or teaching was largely limited to explanation and a little modeling rather than including systematic instruction, followed by guided practice, teacher monitoring, and independent practice as suggested by Rosenshine and Stevens (1984).

Rereading

Romanes (1884), who conducted the first study about reading to be published in English, concluded that for adult readers full comprehension necessitated two readings. Yoakam (1921) concurred that a single reading was not enough and suggested that later experimenters investigate the efficiency of various rereadings. About 6 percent of all the later studies fell into this category. Subsequent investigators most frequently compared these repeated readings of the same material with a variety of study skills, such as summarizing, notetaking, outlining, and underlining. In most of the studies, rereading alone (not in combination with one of the study skills) appeared to be the best technique for improving reading comprehension. A few studies showed no significant differences, and a few favored a given study skill–summarizing in particular.

Reading Practice

The major emphasis in these studies was on extensive reading, sometimes assigned in texts and sometimes in recreational reading. The notion was that practice alone would improve comprehension. Some of the investigators encouraged students to read extensively in class or at home, frequently in conjunction with other approaches. Most had students read easy and interesting materials, although Stone and Colvin (1920), who worked with college students, were convinced that the intensive reading of a difficult book was a vital force in promoting comprehension.

Some of the researchers who tested the exercise method of teaching reading comprehension also included wide reading in their studies. The bulk of these studies were published during the 1920s and 1930s. Oliver (1973) and Wolf and Mikulecky (1978) pitted sustained silent reading (SSR) against skills work to note which would benefit reading comprehension the most. There were no significant differences in either study, although Oliver's results favored SSR.

Study Skills

Over 10 percent of all the studies surveyed were focused on the teaching of study skills as a means of improving reading comprehension. In some of the studies, varied techniques for organizing what is read and for locating information were taught and compared with regard to reading comprehension. In a large number of studies, specific techniques (summarizing, outlining, notetaking, and underlining) were compared against one another or against rereading. As indicated earlier, rereading was frequently the victor. Rarely was it clear in a study whether the subjects knew how to summarize or outline or underline. In other words, the techniques were compared in regard to improving reading comprehension without a period of instruction on how to summarize or outline or underline.

Today there appears to be a renewed interest in summarizing, perhaps as a result of the emphasis on writing and on whole language. There seems to be some promise that teaching summarizing will generate comprehension. Bean and Steenwyk (1984) and Rinehart, Stahl, and Erickson (1986) point toward the improvement of reading comprehension through teaching students how to summarize.

Two early researchers emphasized observation by discovering the study methods used by subjects and then demonstrating the effectiveness of consciousness about study methodology in promoting reading comprehension. Beauchamp (1923) observed the study methods of his eighth graders and then devised, after many trials and errors, a study plan for reading physical science material. He seemed to have included aspects of SQ3R, text structure, and self-monitoring long before these formally emerged. Helseth (1926) observed daily for eight months the study methods of seventh and eighth graders in a U.S. history class. She noted how a process/product approach—placing emphasis on process in attaining a good product—enhanced comprehension. It seems interesting to note that the experimental research movement in education overshadowed this type of research for many years, and only now are we concluding that more naturalistic inquiry is important.

Instrument Presentations

Instruments were introduced into reading instruction primarily to increase rates of reading without risking a loss in comprehension. The studies considered in this monograph, however, are based on the assumption that the use of such instruments can increase comprehension as well. The studies reviewed included instruments used with groups as well as with individuals. Instruments ranged from tachistoscopic devices to various types of pacers. The earliest pacing device, the Metronoscope (used in the 1930s), was not represented in any study focused on comprehension improvement. The first studies dealing with reading comprehension instruction appeared to feature the use of the Harvard Films (Dearborn & Wilking, 1941) and the Reading Pacemaker (Westover, 1946). The remainder were published in the 1960s and were used primarily at the college and high school levels, although two researchers used fifth grade subjects. The most frequent finding was that using the instruments increased speed of reading and generated some interest in the training process, but did not effect significant differences in reading comprehension when compared with varied control situations.

No studies were found from the late 1960s to the present in which instruments were used for improving reading comprehension. The computer, of course, features software related to reading comprehension, but through the middle of 1987 no studies were evident that linked computer use to the intentional teaching of reading comprehension.

Word Study

Seven studies over the years (one in 1956, one in 1966, four in 1979-1980, and one in 1986) concentrated on using some type of word study in the improvement of reading comprehension from the primary grades through college. The approach showed promise in a college level study by McDonald and Pauk (1956), who concentrated on both word derivations and vocabulary in context with significant results across three semesters. The studies reported in 1966 and 1979-1980 did not show significant results. However, Wixson (1986) reported enhanced comprehension for children who worked with a dictionary in prelearning unfamiliar vocabulary. This area of study, ambiguous as the research results appear to be, needs further exploration since the teaching of vocabulary in advance of reading is such a prevalent concept in the literature.

Oral Presentations

Although the emphasis was on oral reading in the years prior to 1920, oral reading was valued for itself rather than as a means of improving comprehension. From 1918 through 1964, at least in the research reports focused on the teaching of reading comprehension, there were no studies that involved oral reading or other kinds of oral presentations as techniques for improving reading comprehension. Since 1965, there have been 16 studies, all sharing an oral component as a means of improving reading comprehension. Frequently, these investigations were concentrated on special populations (limited English speaking, blind, educable mentally handicapped), but a number were based on the notion that listening would benefit normal disabled readers or that it was a better means of helping those with auditory discrimination problems.

Presentations ranged from oral-aural and audiovisual approaches with Spanish-speaking elementary school subjects (mixed results) to the neurological impress method (mixed results) to the apparently more promising technique of repeated readings of taped literature (Laffey, Kelly, & Perry, 1980). Holmes (1985) developed a strategy for teaching inferential comprehension through an oral questioning, oral reading, and listening approach; there was no significant difference between the control and experimental group, but the strategy itself seems worth further testing.

Schema Activation

Although schema theory as a formal concept was unknown until recent years, the majority of the researchers who conducted investigations of the improvement of reading instruction through the years concentrated on schema activation. From 1918 through the present, investigators have been interested in creating a close interaction between the reader and the writer. This always involves some type of stimulation and mobilization of prior knowledge for use upon the reading task. As far back as 1921, Yoakam found that a test of prior knowledge given before reading improved comprehension. Wright (1929) used such a test to ascertain in advance what students knew in order to learn what they gained after the reading. This notion has been discussed recently by Johnston (1984, pp. 154-155).

In the first study concerned with improving reading comprehension, Bird (1918) helped college students learn about the difficult parts of a text they were to read with enough success to have her wonder why contemporaries had students read difficult assignments without preorganization. Stone and Colvin (1920), using an activity external to the content but pertinent to the task, had college students think about and discuss factors related to undertaking a course wherein they did a lot of reading with the goal of improving study abilities. Springsteed (1925) successfully engaged younger students in a number of prereading activities in order to "increase, vivify, and intensify the pupil's knowledge and experience of that which he was about to read" (p. 49).

An interesting technique was introduced by Germane in 1921: the presentation of two paragraphs of a general nature about the topic to be studied. It did not prove to be useful; Germane found questions raised prior to reading showed better results. In 1927, Gatto combined prequestions and shorter selections before study with excellent results. Ausubel (1960) is credited with the concept of introducing this type of shorter selection prior to studying a longer selection; he called the technique an advance organizer. Subsequent studies with advance organizers have shown mixed results; the technique seemed most successful with older students.

Other kinds of advance organizers or preorganizers were used in relation to reading comprehension improvement from 1918 to 1942, with a hiatus from 1943 into the latter part of the 1960s. Ausubel, of course, spurred a number of studies. Earle's (1969) structured overview – a mapping of concept relationships in the material to be read – was tried by a few investigators during the 1970s with mixed results, although recent researchers have found significant results for the treatment group using advanced organizers and structured overviews.

Other researchers have tried preoutlines, the provision of background information, preview summaries, and purposes and objectives with ambivalent results. A technique often used recently is semantic mapping or "webbing" prior to reading (Sinatra, Stahl-Gemake, & Berg, 1984; Tillema, 1983). The technique seems to work best with poor readers, poorly organized material, or difficult text. Schustack and Anderson (1979) indicated that stimulating or providing prior knowledge often resulted in reader bias consistent with the prior knowledge.

Another type of schema activation, adjunct questions, is included in this section on the methodology of schema activation. The authors of this monograph considered any type of question as activating the readers' schemata at some level. We also felt that schema activation was the intent of the investigators who designed studies concerned with adjunct questions, simulation, and embedded study aids such as illustrations and headings. It is conceivable that they might also be included in the methodology of study skills.

The use of adjunct questions was introduced by Frase (1967), who conducted a number of studies from 1967 to 1971. He found that postquestions generally were either equivalent to questions in other positions or, in some studies, appeared to influence comprehension more than prequestions or questions inserted in various places in text. In 1942, Golden found no significant differences between pre and postquestions in relation to reading comprehension. Researchers interested in techniques for improving reading comprehension have long wondered whether to introduce questions. It seems that the presence of questions in any position enabled comprehension. The present emphasis on student-generated questions seems to have merit; studies focused on this area have, in the main, improved reading comprehension, at least within the confines of the given studies.

Other schema activation techniques that usually resulted in the treatment groups doing significantly better than the control groups were simulation games to teach superordinate ideas (Cohen & Bradley, 1977), creative dramatics (Henderson & Shanker,

1978), and embedded study aids (Manzo, 1979; Meeks, 1979). Embedded aids, in addition to questions, consisted of illustrations or headings inserted at some point in text.

Text Structure

The methodology of text structure is often associated with schema activation, but here we wanted to stress the teaching of the authors' schemata; of course, in successful comprehension, the readers' schemata will interact with the text structure as illustrated in several recent studies. Although several earlier investigators (Center & Persons, 1937; Dearborn & Wilking, 1941; McCallister, 1942; Persons, 1934; Salisbury, 1935) placed emphases on organizational patterns and some syntactic features in text, the notion of using text structure to teach reading comprehension is relatively recent. Researchers of the 1960s and early 1970s conducted a number of studies with the cloze procedure as a way of having readers understand the structure of text. The techniques of surveying material and/or learning about paragraph patterns and connectives in advance of reading were utilized, as well as the teaching of plot complexities and story grammar.

In the 1970s and 1980s, researchers often manipulated text to ascertain how to facilitate reading comprehension. In some studies, the structure of the text was analyzed, changed, or altered in some way, and then given to readers to determine in which form it could best be processed. Investigators found that training in some type of syntactic manipulation often proved significant on measures of syntactic maturity but did not give any evidence of facilitating reading comprehension (Mavrogenes & Padak, 1982; Soltis & Pflaum, 1979). Other researchers found that the teaching of expository and/or narrative text structure appears to benefit reading comprehension for many types and levels of learners (Carrell, 1985; Slater, 1985; Taylor & Beach, 1984).

Armbruster, Anderson, and Ostertag (1987) found that teaching fifth grade students to recognize and summarize problem/solution text passages improved comprehension of social studies material. Geva (1983) conducted an interesting study with community college students, combining prior knowledge–the readers' schemata—with the authors' text structure through flowcharting. She found the less skilled readers' ability "to recognize text structure through flowcharting transferred to more careful reading of expository texts" (p. 384). Aspects of text structure appear to have been worthwhile as a means of improving reading comprehension across time; the efforts of today seem especially noteworthy.

Monitoring

Monitoring or self-monitoring is an approach to improving reading comprehension that promotes metacognition or the ability of readers to become conscious of what they know and to use what they know about language structure and content as they interact with text. The assumption is that such metacognitive activity will result in improved reading comprehension. In the past, when metacognition was an unknown term to most researchers, a relatively large group of researchers who concentrated on reading exercises as the means of improving reading comprehension also encouraged students to improve by showing, posting, and discussing reading scores. They had students graph their progress and hold self-analysis conferences.

For instance, Stone and Colvin (1920) asked college students what they did when they studied and what factors they believed were important in study. A list was compiled and students rated themselves from fair to excellent for each study technique. They filled out the form again after a course concentrated on study techniques plus extensive intensive reading. Helseth (1926) found that eighth graders who were trained to pay more attention to methods of study than to recitation of facts became better comprehenders. Hill (1964) worked with college students who were poor readers and found the most success in comprehension after students were permitted to monitor their errors by rereading and correction. Students appreciated the opportunity to revise their comprehension products; they said the opportunity was unique in their school experience.

The emphasis on metacognition and strategies for developing it are relatively recent. There has been much more discussion than actual studies, but there does seem to be a trend toward teaching monitoring strategies, often in collaboration with text structure and schema activation strategies. Brown and Palincsar (1982) and Palincsar and Brown (1984), for example, found that corrective feedback followed by strategy training was successful in teaching readers to paraphrase the main idea and hypothesize about the content of subsequent segments of a passage. Garner et al. (1984) taught elementary students a text lookback technique that they were able to employ successfully over a five-day period. At this point, self-monitoring seems successful with students in the intermediate grades and above.

Summary and Concluding Remarks

Eleven categories of methods for teaching or improving reading comprehension emerged from our review of twentieth century research: exercises and drills, teacher-directed skill lessons, rereading, reading practice, study skills, instrument presentations, word study, oral presentations, schema activation, text structure, and monitoring. The methods described have been used mostly with poor readers, although several investigators focused on average and above average readers as well. The methods have been used in regular classroom settings and in remedial pullout situations. Studies ranged from skill development isolated from the curriculum to programs that attempted skill transfer to the content areas.

A number of investigators, from the 1920s through the 1950s and then again in the 1970s, believed in and taught reading and study skills within content areas as opposed to teaching reading skills separately and then making application to content areas. For instance, based on his work with ninth graders in science, Jacobsen (1933) stated: "These data warrant the conclusion that giving reading instruction in the field in which the content is to be mastered is superior to giving it in another subject matter field and expecting the ability to transfer to a content field" (p. 78).

Some of the methods used in the past, and then not continued or refined, may be worth exploring today. The most recent trends (even though each has a history) in the teaching of reading comprehension–schema activation, utilizing text structure, and self-monitoring–seem to be worth much more research activity, particularly in relation to the development of viable strategies for improving reading comprehension. Researchers today provide a dimension not frequently utilized in the past—that of direct instruction through the development of strategies aimed toward metacognitive awareness and developed reciprocally by teachers and students. Only two reports were focused on computer-assisted instruction and the teaching of reading comprehension. Whether the computer and its software one day will play a role in this direct effort to improve reading comprehension remains an unknown at this time.

References

Alderman, G.H. Improving comprehension ability in silent reading. *Journal of Educational Research,* 1926, *13,* 11-21.

Armbruster, B.B., Anderson, T.H., and Ostertag, J. Does text structure/summarization instruction facilitate learning from expository text? *Reading Research Quarterly,* 1987, *22,* 331-346.

Ausubel, D. The use of advance organizers in the learning and retention of meaningful verbal material. *Journal of Educational Research,* 1960, *51,* 267-272.

Bean, T.W., and Steenwyk, F.L. The effect of three forms of summarization instruction on sixth graders' summary writing and comprehension. *Journal of Reading Behavior,* 1984, *16,* 297-306.

Beauchamp, W.L. A preliminary experimental study of technique in the mastery of subject matter in elementary physical science. In *Studies in secondary education 1,* Supplementary Educational Monograph No 24. Chicago, IL: Department of Education, University of Chicago, 1923, 47-87.

Bird, G.E. An experiment in focalization. *School and Society,* 1918, *8,* 569-570.

Bond, G.L., and Dykstra, R. The cooperative research program in first grade reading instruction. *Reading Research Quarterly,* 1967, *2,* 5-141.

Brown, A.L., and Palincsar, A.S. Inducing strategic learning from texts by means of informed, self-control training. *Topics in Learning and Learning Disabilities,* 1982, *2,* 1-17.

Carrell, P.I. Facilitating ESL reading by teaching text structure. *TESOL Quarterly,* 1985, *19,* 727-752.

Center, S.S., and Persons, G.L. *Teaching high school students to read: A study of retardation in reading.* New York: Appleton-Century, 1937.

Cohen, R.B., and Bradley, R.H. Teaching superordinate concepts with simulation games. *Alberta Journal of Educational Research,* 1977, *23,* 298-304.

Dearborn, W.F., and Wilking, S.V. Improving the reading of college freshmen. *School Review,* 1941, *49,* 668-678.

Durrell, D. Development of comprehension and interpretation. In N.B. Henry (Ed.), *Reading in the elementary school.* Forty-Eighth Yearbook of the National Society for the Study of Education, Part 2. Chicago, IL: University of Chicago Press, 1949, 193-204.

Earle, R.A. Reading and mathematics: Research in the classroom. In H.A. Robinson and E.L. Thomas (Eds.), *Fusing reading skills and content.* Newark, DE: International Reading Association, 1969.

Frase, L.T. Learning from prose material, length of passage, knowledge of results, and position of questions. *Journal of Educational Psychology,* 1967, *58,* 266-272.

Froese, V., and Kurushima, S. The effects of sentence expansion practice on the reading comprehension and writing ability of third graders. In M.L. Kamil and A.J. Moe (Eds.), *Reading research: Studies and applications.* Twenty-Eighth Yearbook of the National Reading Conference. Clemson, NC: National Reading Conference, 1979, 95-99.

Garner, R., Hare, V.C., Alexander, P., Haynes, J., and Winograd, P. Inducing use of a text lookback strategy among unsuccessful readers. *American Educational Research Journal,* 1984, *21,* 789-798.

Gates, A.I., and Van Alstyne, D. The general and specific effects of training in reading with observations on the experimental technique. *Teachers College Record,* 1924, *25,* 98-123.

Gatto, F.M. The effect of parallel reading in history. *University of Pittsburgh School of Education Journal,* 1927, *2,* 3-8.

Germane, C.E. Outlining and summarizing compared with rereading as methods of studying. In G.M. Whipple (Ed.), *Silent reading.* Twentieth Yearbook of the National Society for the Study of Education, Part 2. Bloomington, IL: Public School Publishing, 1921, 103-112.

Geva, E. Facilitating reading comprehension through flowcharting. *Reading Research Quarterly,* 1983, *18,* 384-405.

Golden, M.L. Reading guided questions versus careful reading followed by questions. *Journal of Educational Psychology,* 1942, *33,* 463-468.

Gray, W.S. The relation of silent reading to economy in education. In G.M. Whipple (Ed.), *Second report of the committee on minimal essentials in elementary school subjects.* Sixteenth Yearbook of the National Society for the Study of Education, Part 1. Bloomington, IL: Public School Publishing, 1917, 17-32.

Helseth, I.O. *Children's thinking: A study of the thinking done by a group of grade children when encouraged to ask questions about United States history.* Contributions to Education No. 209. New York: Bureau of Publications, Teachers College, Columbia University, 1926.

Henderson, L.C., and Shanker, J.L. The use of interpretive dramatics versus basal reader workbooks for developing comprehension. *Reading World,* 1978, *17,* 239-242.

Henry, N.B. (Ed.). *The measurement of understanding.* Forty-Fifth Yearbook of the National Society for the Study of Education, Part 1. Chicago, IL: University of Chicago Press, 1946.

Henry, N.B. (Ed.). *Reading in the elementary school.* Forty-Eighth Yearbook of the National Society for the Study of Education, Part 2. Chicago, IL: University of Chicago Press, 1949.

Hill, W.R. Influence of direction upon the reading flexibility of advanced college readers. In E.L. Thurstone and L.E. Hafner (Eds.), *New concepts in college-adult reading.* Thirteenth Yearbook of the National Reading Conference. Milwaukee, WI: National Reading Conference, 1964.

Holmes, B.C. The effects of strategy and sequenced materials on the inferential comprehension of disabled readers. *Journal of Learning Disabilities,* 1985, *18,* 542-546.

Jacobson, P.B. Two experiments with work type reading exercises in ninth grade. *University of Iowa Studies in Education,* 1933, *8,* 1-85.

Johnston, P.H. Assessment in reading. In P.D. Pearson (Ed.), *Handbook of reading research.* New York: Longman, 1984.

Laffey, J.L., Kelly, D., and Perry, B. The effect of repeated reading of taped literature on reading achievement. In M.L. Kamil and A.J. Moe (Eds.), *Perspectives on reading research and instruction.* Twenty-Ninth Yearbook of the National Reading Conference. Washington, DC: National Reading Conference, 1980, 189-193.

Lowerre, G.F., and Scandura, J.M. Conceptually based development and evaluation of individualized materials for critical reading based on logical inference. *Reading Research Quarterly,* 1974, *9,*186-205.

Maddison, J.M., and Rimmington, G.T. The improvement of reading: An experimental study. *Canadian Education and Research Digest,* 1966, *6,* 188-190.
Manzo, A.V. Imbedded aids to readers: Alternative to traditional textual material. *New England Reading Association Journal,* 1979, *14,* 13-18.
Mavrogenes, N.A., and Padak, N.D. The reading road to writing. *Journal of Educational Research,* 1982, *75,* 354-359.
McCallister, J.M. College instruction in reading. *Phi Delta Kappan,* 1942, *24,* 311-313.
McCullough, C.M. What does research reveal about practices in teaching reading? *English Journal,* 1957, *46,* 475-490.
McDonald, A.S., and Pauk, W.J. Teaching college freshmen to read. *Phi Delta Kappan,* 1956, *38,* 104-109.
Meeks, J.W. Imbedded aids to readers: An alternative textbook approach. *Reading Improvement,* 1979, *16,* 95-98.
Miles, D.H. Can the high-school pupil improve his reading ability? *Journal of Educational Research,* 1926, *14,* 88-98.
Oliver, M.E. The effect of high intensity practice on reading comprehension. *Reading Improvement,* 1973, *10,* 16-18.
Palincsar, A.S., and Brown, A.L. Reciprocal teaching of comprehension fostering and comprehension activities. *Cognition and Instruction,* 1984, *1,* 117-175.
Persons, G.L. Silent reading with first-term pupils in the Theodore Roosevelt High School. *High Points in the Work of the High Schools in the City of New York,* 1934, *16,* 5-15.
Rinehart, S.D., Stahl, S.A., and Erickson, L.G. Some effects of summarization training on reading and studying. *Reading Research Quarterly,* 1986, *21,* 422-438.
Romanes, G.J. *Mental evolution in animals.* New York: J. Appleton, 1884.
Rosenshine, B., and Stevens, R. Classroom instruction in reading. In P.D. Pearson (Ed.), *Handbook of reading research.* New York: Longman, 1984.
Salisbury, R. A study of the transfer effects of training in logical organization. *Journal of Educational Research,* 1934, *38,* 241-254. Also reported as Some effects of training in outlining. *English Journal,* 1935, *24,* 111-116.
Schustack, M.W., and Anderson, J.R. Effects of analogy to prior knowledge on memory for new information. *Journal of Verbal Learning and Verbal Behavior,* 1979, *18,* 565-583.
Sinatra, R.C., Stahl-Gemake, J., and Berg, D.N. Improving reading comprehension of disabled readers through semantic mapping. *The Reading Teacher,* 1984, *38,* 22-29.
Slama, E.A. A silent reading poster lesson. *Chicago Schools Journal,* 1923, *6,* 142-144.
Slater, W.H. Teaching expository text structure with structural organizers. *Journal of Reading,* 1985, *28,* 712-718.
Smith, N.B. *American reading instruction.* Newark, DE: International Reading Association, 1965, 1986.
Soltis, J.M., and Pflaum, S. The effect of instruction in connectives on reading comprehension. *Reading World,* 1979, *19,* 179-184.
Springsteed, C.B. Improving speed and comprehension in reading. *Journal of Educational Method,* 1925, *5,* 48-52.
Stone, C.W., and Colvin, C. "How to study" as a source of motive in educational psychology. *Journal of Educational Psychology,* 1920, *11,* 348-354.
Taylor, B.M. Teaching middle-grade students to read for main ideas. In J.A. Niles and R.V. Lalek (Eds.), *Solving problems in literacy: Learners, teachers, and researchers.* Thirty-Fifth Yearbook of the National Reading Conference. Rochester, NY: National Reading Conference, 1986, 99-104.
Taylor, B.M., and Beach, R.W. The effects of text structure instruction on middle-grade students' comprehension and production of expository text. *Reading Research Quarterly,* 1984, *19,* 134-146.
Tillema, H. Webteaching: Sequencing of subject matter in relation to prior knowledge of pupils. *Instructional Science,* 1983, *12,* 321-332.

Westover, F.L. *Controlled eye movements versus practice exercises in reading.* Contributions to Education No. 917. New York: Bureau of Publications, Teachers College, Columbia University, 1946.

Whipple, G.M. (Ed.). *Report of the national committee on reading.* Twenty-Fourth Yearbook of the National Society for the Study of Education, Part 1. Bloomington, IL: Public School Publishing, 1925.

Whipple, G.M. (Ed.). *The teaching of reading: A second report.* Thirty-Sixth Yearbook of the National Society for the Study of Education, Part 1. Bloomington, IL: Public School Publishing, 1937.

Wixson, K.K. Vocabulary instruction and children's comprehension of basal stories. *Reading Research Quarterly,* 1986, *21,* 317-329.

Wolf, A.E., and Mikulecky, L. Effects of uninterrupted sustained silent reading and of reading skills instruction on changes in secondary students' reading attitudes and achievement. In P.D. Pearson and J. Hansen (Eds.), *Reading: Disciplined inquiry in process and practice.* Twenty-Seventh Yearbook of the National Reading Conference, 1978, *27,* 226-228.

Wright, L.B. The value of a motivated assignment: An experiment in directed study. *University of Pittsburgh School of Education Journal,* 1929, *4,* 64-67.

Yoakam, G.A. The effect of a single reading. In G.M. Whipple (Ed.), *Report of the society's committee on silent reading.* Twentieth Yearbook of the National Society for the Study of Education, Part 2. Bloomington, IL: Public School Publishing, 1921, 90-102.

4

Conclusions and Suggestions

In this chapter, trends in American reading comprehension instruction (as reflected in nineteenth century documents and twentieth century research) are summarized, questions are raised, and problems are noted. We first highlight what we consider to be the most important trends in reading comprehension instruction over time. Then, since it appeared to be a different concept at different times and in the minds of different investigators, we consider the nature of reading comprehension and its inferred influence on reading comprehension instruction. Next we present promising findings followed by suggestions for future directions. The chapter ends with remarks about reading comprehension instruction.

Trends in American Reading Comprehension Instruction

In many respects, it is risky to declare trends in reading comprehension instruction across the nineteenth and twentieth centuries. Trends imply absolutes. Declaration of movement from one emphasis to another suggests that certain kinds of comprehension instruction occurred during particular periods, and *only* during those periods. In reality, such absolutes did not exist. Movements over time merely reflected changes in predominance or focus, with different emphases generally overlapping greatly. One of the most striking lessons we learned from our work was that for nearly every concept most educators would now consider utterly modern, there were early twentieth century predecessors. Yet as we developed this monograph, we became aware of changes in emphases. Here are the major shifts we discerned:

1. The most dramatic change occurred toward the beginning of the twentieth century—the instructional shift from using and improving oral reading as a means of affecting "meaning-getting" to a focus on comprehension during silent reading.

2. There was a movement from instruction involving external control over student comprehension to internal student control. This was reflected in a former emphasis on the use of instruments, worksheets and workbooks, kits, or other materials to a more recent interest in affecting readers' mental processes so they might gain self-control over their own reading comprehension strategies.

3. Instruction moved from drill on the *what* of comprehension (e.g., using skills books to practice getting the main idea) to learning about the *how* and *why* of comprehension (e.g., learning how to make inferences while reading).

4. Formerly, instructional emphasis was placed on teaching the "subskills of comprehension" (e.g., learning about sequence in texts by practicing sequence exercises), whereas more recently, instruction has focused on holistic comprehension strategies (e.g., coping better with the ideas in a given text through learning how to summarize).

5. Instruction seems to be moving from little direct teaching to specific and direct teaching followed by supervised and independent practice.

Overall, these patterns appear to reflect: (1) an evolving view of comprehension as a holistic and unitary process affected by the teacher, the learner, the context, the purposes for reading, and the materials to be read; (2) an increased concern over the years for the mental processes involved in comprehension and the extent to which such processes can be strengthened—a concern that in all likelihood also reflects the trend in psychology away from behaviorism and toward cognition; (3) an increased recognition of the role teachers may play in the advancement of their students' reading comprehension; and (4) an increased recognition of the extent to which students can direct their own learning.

Inferred Views of Reading Comprehension and Their Effects

One problem impinging on investigations concerned with reading comprehension instruction relates to definitions of reading comprehension. During the latter part of the nineteenth century the term *meanings* evolved, followed in the first part of the twentieth century by *understanding what one reads.* The prevailing view of reading comprehension for many years thereafter appeared to be that it was the sum of multiple parts; comprehension was a product—what you ended up with after reading.

The summative view of reading comprehension was reflected in early twentieth century research not only through the kinds of instruction that were studied, but also through the outcome measures used in the studies. Standardized tests of silent reading were typical; they usually consisted of passages to be read followed by multiple-choice questions aimed at main ideas, details, and sometimes conclusions and inferences. Researchers occasionally employed measures that required summarizing or composing an outline or an essay.

In recent times, with reading comprehension defined as holistic or unitary, the process of comprehension has received more attention than the product. Many of today's theorists, researchers, and practitioners view reading comprehension as task specific; that is, it cannot be defined universally, for it is almost always connected to a given task and/or purpose for reading in a given situation. The holistic view of reading comprehension was reflected in investigations such as those that concentrated on background knowledge of the reader and the structure of large units of reading materials, as well as assessments carefully tuned to the tasks at hand.

Promising Findings

In reviewing the body of research explored in the preparation of this monograph, we realized that there were a vast number of individual pieces that we could not seem to put together to form a cohesive whole. Even though we could group studies into a variety of broad categories, there was no design that might point toward overall plans for classroom implementation. We did discover a number of diverse but apparently effective models for developing overall procedures for improving reading comprehension that ought to be considered by future investigators:

• Beauchamp's (1923) study plan in elementary physical science, because it seemed highly successful and illuminated a study plan that apparently was never replicated;

• Helseth's (1926) ethnographic approach to developing metacognitive abilities in United States history as another example of a valuable study that was never replicated, and also as an early example of the current emphasis on process and naturalistic study;

• Colwell's (1982) model for processing ideas, which shows promise as a plan for transfer to multiple learning situations;

• Davey and Porter's (1982) emphasis on pupil interaction with text, an approach that demonstrates the learner as an active comprehender; and

• the emphasis on metacognitive strategies begun by Brown and Palincsar (1982), a way of helping readers develop a consciousness of their own reading processes and enabling transfer from one context to another.

We are aware that other plans and overall strategies exist, but because of the limitations we placed on our search of the literature, we did not include such models unless they were immediately attached to instructional strategies.

We did feel that the literature illuminated some specific ways of teaching reading comprehension that should be considered by researchers and teachers. The groupings of methods that follow were largely successful and appear to be strategies that can be used in whole language programs.

Summarizing. A number of researchers in the 1920s and 1930s (Germane, 1921; Newlun, 1920; Salisbury, 1934; Springsteed, 1925; Witty & Lehman, 1927) found some type of summarizing valuable in developing reading comprehension. After many experiments, Germane learned that his form of summarizing (listing important points after reading) was useful when combined with questions raised prior to reading. Salisbury documented the value of summarizing in converting student-generated outlines to summaries. Now, again, in the 1980s, Rinehart, Stahl, and Erickson (1986) and Bean and Steenwyk (1984) conclude, from their studies with middle graders, that summarization training can be effective in improving reading comprehension. Particularly in relation to the whole language teaching of today, where writing and superordinate-subordinate relationships are emphasized, it seems reasonable to pursue a variety of ways of using summarizing for teaching reading comprehension.

Student-generated questions or organizational aids. A number of investigators found that when students generated their own questions related to the reading material or composed their own headings for sections of text, comprehension improved (Davey & McBride, 1986; Dee-Lucas & DiVesta, 1980; Doctorow, Witrock, & Marks, 1978; Prosser, 1979; Ritchie, 1985). Helfeldt and Lalik (1976, 1979) reported the most success in reading comprehension when questions were generated in a reciprocal teacher-student setting. Davey and McBride (1986) found that students trained to generate questions improved in their answers to inferential questions. Since schema activation seems most viable when placed in the hands of the learner, student generation of questions and headings as means of improving reading comprehension appears to be an open avenue for exploration. Also, the work of Helfeldt and Lalik points toward the value of collaborative learning as an aspect of teaching reading comprehension.

Preknowledge. From 1918 (Bird) to the present, researchers have been fascinated with the influence of preknowledge on what was to be read or studied. Investigators have designed studies in which only prior knowledge has been stimulated or in which prior knowledge has been combined with new information introduced before reading or studying a selection. Those researchers who tapped prior knowledge alone generally tended to report improved comprehension. When prior knowledge was combined with a structure to introduce new information, as in advance organizers, structured overviews, and mapping of some kind, results were mixed with no clearcut direction. Although Schustack and Anderson (1979) warned of a reader bias consistent with the prior knowledge, the area still appears viable for further exploration, particularly in light of the success that occurs when students generate their own organizations of prior and new knowledge. Geva's (1983) technique of having students flowchart prior knowledge and text structure seems an interesting and useful approach to consider.

Text structure. Utilizing the schema of the writer—text structure—in combination with the schema of the reader appears to be a promising direction for research, according to the results in the studies reviewed in this monograph. Although a few investigators in the 1930s and 1940s (Center & Persons, 1937; Dearborn & Wilking, 1941; McCallister, 1930; Persons, 1934; Salisbury, 1934) placed emphasis on syntactical features and organizational patterns of text, using text structure as an aid for teaching reading comprehension is a contemporary effort. For example, Armbruster, Anderson, and Ostertag (1987) found that teaching fifth grade students to recognize and summarize problem/solution text passages improved comprehension of social studies material. Slater's (1985) ninth graders' comprehension improved when they were given information about the organization of a passage they were to read. Carrell (1985) reported that training on the top level rhetorical organization of expository texts significantly increased the amount of information that intermediate level ESL students recalled. Spiegel and Fitzgerald (1986) concluded that direct instruction in story structure with less able fourth grade pupils resulted in significant improvement on comprehension tasks and on the production of more complex and more fully formed studies.

Monitoring. Stone and Colvin (1920) and Helseth (1926) made their students aware of their own study techniques and found the process profitable. From that time until the late 1970s, little attention was paid (at least in studies of teaching reading comprehension) to promoting metacognitive activity or self-monitoring as a technique for increasing reading comprehension. Brown's seminal work in strategies and training began in 1975 and continues today. Baker and Brown (1984) described three main features in metacognitive training: (1) training and practice in the use of task-specific strategies (skills training); (2) instruction in the orchestration, overseeing, and monitoring of these skills (self-regulation training); and (3) information concerning the significance and outcome of these activities and their range of utility (awareness training) (p. 381). This whole area of metacognitive awareness training, self-monitoring, and self-regulation would appear to be significant in guiding students toward independence as readers.

Future Directions

With the emphasis today on viewing the processes of comprehending within given tasks in specific contexts, future researchers might profit by observing the comprehending processes of individual students as they read for varied purposes in a variety of situations, and then, within the same study, following those observations with specific teaching methods based on the insights gained. As far back as 1926, Helseth urged the use of a process/product approach as a means of improving reading comprehension.

Another way of learning more about comprehending and comprehension is to view classroom dynamics as students are asked to comprehend. Mosenthal (1984) challenged:

> the assumption that the results from formal experimental situations provide us with valid explanations of how children read and learn to read in classroom lessons....[He] argued that while reading researchers have tended to define reading comprehension primarily in terms of text, task, and subject contexts, the most important context influencing reading comprehension in classroom lessons may be the interaction between the teacher and the students (p. 17).

No reports were found in which the teaching of reading comprehension was assessed based on varied purposes and materials within the contexts of particular classrooms, although the results of the First Grade Studies in the late 1960s pointed toward teachers as more important than materials (Bond & Dykstra, 1967). It is evident that researchers are now exploring the subtleties of interactions among teachers and students as factors influencing reading instruction; none at this point have dealt with such factors in relation to an actual study of teaching reading comprehension. Future researchers might contribute profitable insights and directions by designing studies in which teacher/student interactions are tracked and observed prior to, during, and following the teaching of a lesson directed toward improving reading comprehension.

There appears to be a need for more insights about the teaching of evaluation and more acceptance and analysis of divergent production. Rosenblatt's (1978) transactional theory of a literary work suggests the beginnings of a model for teaching reading comprehension that subsequent investigators might consider.

Alternative outcome measures might be considered in future research. Past researchers have depended mainly upon multiple-choice, completion, or cloze tests; we might well ask if such tests measure comprehension in total (perhaps an unrealistic objective) or if they each measure just certain aspects of comprehension. Are "aesthetic" responses to literature measurable through objective questions? Is it necessary to organize information in writing in order to really comprehend?

Other assessment instruments in addition to outcome measures also should be considered. For example, teacher awareness of the background knowledge of students—including their degrees of expertise in handling different text structures—would appear to be an important consideration. However, when informal tests are utilized, if consumers of research are to have any confidence in the results, it seems obligatory for the investigator to report, at least, that the tests were piloted successfully and/or modified when necessary.

Contemporary theorists and writers are deeply concerned about transfer of skills, knowledge, or processes taught. Yet few researchers have assessed transfer in their studies. It well might be that procedures effective with narrative materials in one situation would not transfer to narrative in another, or that the use of such procedures with expository materials might not be profitable or might need modification. Or maybe interactions with one teacher in a given context will affect the use of a given strategy with another teacher in a different situation. Research is needed that describes the teaching of a strategy in one situation and its effects as it is transferred to other tasks, other contexts, and novel situations, as well as for a new set of purposes. In reality, reading comprehension can be thought of only as a portrait drawn across a variety of purposes and tasks, using different types of materials in a multitude of situations.

Investigators should provide a full and adequate analysis of prior research in order to reveal strong rationales for their own work. In addition, the instructional procedures used in studies should be completely and explicitly explained to enable a thorough understanding of what was done and to permit replication. Granted, the limitations of space provided by publishers may be part of the problem, but if we are to learn how to teach reading comprehension in a variety of settings to many levels and types of readers, such information is essential.

Finally, investigations over extended periods are needed. In all probability, lasting comprehension strategies cannot be learned in five days or five weeks. Investigators need to compare—in delayed usage and recall studies—the effect of training time. It seems logical that for students to use study and comprehension strategies independently, enough time must be devoted to helping them become conscious of their strategies so they are able to utilize them in novel situations. Also, longitudinal studies are needed so insights can be gained about the developmental nature of both instructional procedures and specific strategies as they affect and effect learning across age and grade levels.

Concluding Remarks

Although there were a number of promising techniques and strategies reported in the research literature, Durkin's (1979) conclusion, based on her observations of classrooms, was confirmed over the long run: most of the researchers appeared to test much more than they taught. For example, comparing summarizing with underlining without determining students' prior ability to do either or without teaching them both skills in advance of the comparison results in misleading findings unrelated to instruction, although past researchers often concluded from such findings that one teaching technique was better than another. More contemporary researchers consider summarization training to be the better teaching technique, and they have achieved far better and more consistent results in improving reading comprehension.

The definition of teaching, of course, may be as elusive as the definition of comprehension. An environment that fosters collaborative, critical thinking in a variety of situations, with a variety of tasks, and with differing kinds of text, may be more satisfactory for some students than direct teaching. Under any condition, the role of a teacher seems to be a powerful ingredient. In summarizing recent research, Rosenshine and Stevens (1984) reported that teacher-directed initial instruction, instruction in groups, and the maintenance of a strong academic emphasis in the classroom were correlated with reading achievement gain. Future researchers concerned with reading comprehension instruction will find it interesting and challenging to test and compare Rosenshine and Stevens's emphases with the present interest in the collaborative learning movement and the process of learning itself as a metacognitive tool.

As was evident in the review of the literature, a few of the investigators looked at the learning process as a means of teaching reading comprehension. Such studies do show promise in helping us learn more about instruction. Prevailing theory tells us there is much to be learned from observing learners as they use techniques of their own or those they are taught, how they interact with teachers and peers during the process, and how they employ metacognitive strategies.

A number of contemporary investigators are studying reading as both a linguistic and social process embedded in both linguistic and social contexts (Bloome & Green, 1984). In such a paradigm, teachers can become researchers in their own or in their colleagues' classrooms with some assistance from supervisors and/or university personnel. The classroom is the most logical place to note learner strategies as well as learner/learner and teacher/learner interactions in a variety of reading comprehension contexts. Teachers who are trained in research methodology and are eager to try methods of teaching reading comprehension are in a position to assess the effects of process on product. We still have much to learn about reading comprehesion and instruction, but we seem to be headed toward acquiring knowledge that cannot help but benefit the teachers and learners of the future.

References

Armbruster, B.B. , Anderson, T. H., and Ostertag, J. Does text structure/summarization instruction facilitate learning from expository text? *Reading Research Quarterly,* 1987, *22,* 331-346.

Baker, L., and Brown, A.L. Metacognitive skills and reading. In P. D. Pearson (Ed.), *Handbook of reading research.* New York: Longman, 1984.

Bean, T.W., and Steenwyk, F.L. The effect of three forms of summarization instruction on sixth graders' summary writing and comprehension. *Journal of Reading Behavior,* 1984, *16,* 297-306.

Beauchamp, W.L. A preliminary experimental study of technique in the mastery of subject matter in elementary physical science. *Studies in secondary education 1,* Supplementary Educational Monograph No. 24. Chicago, IL: Department of Education, University of Chicago, 1923, 47-87.

Bird, G.E. An experiment in focalization. *School and Society,* 1918, *8,* 569-570.

Bloome, D., and Green, J. Directions in the sociolinguistic study of reading. In P.D. Pearson (Ed.), *Handbook of reading research.* New York: Longman, 1984.

Bond, G.L., and Dykstra, R. The cooperative research program in first grade reading instruction. *Reading Research Quarterly,* 1967, *2,* 5-141.

Brown, A.L. The development of memory: Knowing, knowing about knowing, and knowing how to know. In H.W. Reese (Ed.), *Advances in child development and behavior,* volume 10. New York: Academic Press, 1975.

Brown, A.L., and Palincsar, A.S. Inducing strategic learning from texts by means of informed, self-control training. *Topics in Learning and Learning Disabilities,* 1982, *2,* 1-17.

Carrell, P.L. Facilitating ESL reading by teaching text structure. *TESOL Quarterly,* 1985, *19,* 727-752.

Center, S.S., and Persons, G.L. *Teaching high-school students to read: A study of retardation in reading.* New York: D. Appleton-Century, 1937.

Colwell, C.G. Paragraph processing: A direct-functional-interactive model. *Reading Improvement,* 1982, *19,* 13-24.

Davey, B., and McBride, S. Effects of question-generation training on reading comprehension. *Journal of Educational Psychology,* 1986, *78,* 256-262.

Davey, B., and Porter, S.M. Comprehension-rating: A procedure to assist poor comprehenders. *Journal of Reading,* 1982, *26,* 197-202.

Dearborn, W.F., and Wilking, S.V. Improving the reading of college freshmen. *School Review,* 1941, *49,* 668-678.

Dee-Lucas, K., and DiVesta, F.J. Learner-generated organizational aids: Effects on learning from text. *Journal of Educational Psychology,* 1980, *72,* 304-311.

Doctorow, M., Witrock, M.C., and Marks, C. Generative processes in reading comprehension. *Journal of Educational Psychology,* 1978, *70,* 109-118.

Durkin, D. What classroom observations reveal about reading comprehension instruction. *Reading Research Quarterly,* 1979, *14,* 481-533.

Germane, C.E. Outlining and summarizing compared with rereading as methods of studying. In G. M. Whipple (Ed.), *Report of the society's committee on silent reading.* Twentieth Yearbook of the National Society for the Study of Education, Part 2. Bloomington, IL: Public School Publishing, 1921, 103-113.

Geva, E. Facilitating reading comprehension through flowcharting. *Reading Research Quarterly,* 1983, *18,* 384-405.

Helfeldt, J.P., and Lalik, R. Reciprocal student-teacher questioning. *The Reading Teacher,* 1976, *30,* 283-287.

Helfeldt, J.P., and Lalik, R. Reciprocal student-teacher questioning. In C. Pennock (Ed.), *Reading comprehension at four linguistic levels.* Newark, DE: International Reading Association, 1979, 74-79.

Helseth, I.O. *Children's thinking: A study of the thinking done by a group of grade children when encouraged to ask questions about United States history.* Contributions to Education, No. 209. New York: Bureau of Publications, Teachers College, Columbia University, 1926.

McCallister, J.M. Reading difficulties in studying content subjects. *Elementary School Journal,* 1930, *31,* 191-201.

Mosenthal, P. Reading comprehension research from a classroom perspective. In J. Flood (Ed.), *Promoting reading comprehension.* Newark, DE: International Reading Association, 1984, 16-29.

Newlun, C.O. *Teaching children to summarize in fifth grade history.* Contributions to Education, No. 404. New York: Teachers College, Columbia University, 1930.

Persons, G.L. Silent reading with first-term pupils in the Theodore Roosevelt High School. *High Points in the Work of the High Schools of the City of New York,* 1934, *16,* 5-15.

Prosser, G.V. The role of relevant active questions in learning based upon successive presentations. *Instructional Science,* 1978, *7,* 359-383.

Rinehart, S.D., Stahl, S.A., and Erickson, L.G. Some effects of summarization training on reading and studying. *Reading Research Quarterly,* 1986, *21,* 422-438.

Ritchie, P. The effects of instruction in main idea and question generation. *Reading-Canada-Lecture,* 1985, *3,* 139-146.

Rosenblatt, L.M. *The reader, the text, the poem: The transactional theory of the literary work.* Carbondale, IL: Southern Illinois University Press, 1978.

Rosenshine, B., and Stevens, R. Classroom instruction in reading. In P.D. Pearson (Ed.), *Handbook of reading research.* New York: Longman, 1984.

Salisbury, R. A study of the transfer effects of training in logical organization. *Journal of Educational Research,* 1934, *38,* 241-254.

Schustack, M.W., and Anderson, J.R. Effects of analogy to prior knowledge on memory for new information. *Journal of Verbal Learning and Verbal Behavior,* 1979, *18,* 565-583.

Slater, W.H. Teaching expository text structure with structural organizers. *Journal of Reading,* 1985, *28,* 712-718.

Spiegel, D.L., and Fitzgerald, J. Improving reading comprehension through instruction about story parts. *The Reading Teacher,* 1986, *39,* 676-682.

Springsteed, C.B. Improving speed and comprehension in reading. *Journal of Educational Method,* 1925, *5,* 48-52.

Stone, C.W., and Colvin, C. "How to study" as a source of motive in educational psychology. *Journal of Educational Psychology,* 1920, *11,* 348-354.

Witty, P.A., and Lehman, H.C. Teaching the college student "how to study" education. *Education,* 1927, *48,* 47-56.

Appendix A

Overview of the Research Reports

The complete citation for each of the studies mentioned is listed in the References (Appendix B).

Exercises and Drills

Group 1: Teacher-Designed Material

Hoover (1921) provided drill work (not described) for 568 third graders over a three month period. A nondrill group of 571 apparently continued the "traditional" program. On the Monroe Silent Reading Test, the drill group increased median comprehension scores from 4.0 to 9.0; the nondrill group increased from 3.9 to 7.0.

James (1922) had student teachers help 52 third graders who obtained poor scores on the Picture Supplement Scale of the Burgess. Exercises were similar to the items on the Burgess, although the student teachers devised their own as time went on. The test was administered three additional times during a period of a little more than four months. Results showed an average gain close to grade level through the second administration but a slight regression on the third. In 1924, Lynch constructed a series of lessons imitative of the tasks on the Burgess for 16 eighth graders whose initial group median was fourth grade level. After eight weeks of work, the group scored a median of ninth grade level on the Burgess.

Slama (1923) drilled primary subjects (no *N* nor specific grade levels given) in the reading of directions. After 10 weeks of drill correlated with the regular silent reading work and some group experiences in reading directions, subjects more than doubled their scores on the Haggerty Test in Reading.

Alderman (1923) organized three experimental drill groups from 1,201 fourth through eighth graders to focus on: (1) vocabulary, recording definitions, and writing illustrative sentences; (2) organization and important paragraph ideas in outline form; and (3) retention-reproduction, rapid reading followed by testing. A control group continued their "regular" work. After six weeks, as measured by the Thorndike-McCall Reading Scale, drill groups gained 3.81 points compared with 1.46 for the nondrill, control group. The organization group made the most gain. In 1925, Alderman, now working with 1,933 fourth through eighth graders, used all three variables with one experimental group while a control group carried on the traditional program. Results on the Thorndike-McCall showed only 5 of 75 experimental classes above standard in September; 35 of the 75 were above standard in February. In 1926, Alderman went back to three separate experimental groups drilling on vocabulary, organization, or retention. This time he worked for six weeks with 1,519 fourth through eighth graders. Gains on the Thordike-McCall as well as on the drill exercises themselves were higher for subjects who scored low originally.

Williams and McCabe (1923) raised group consciousness about scores on daily timed drills through the posting of histograms and by urging their 43 fourth grade subjects to improve. Fourteen began with scores on the Monroe that placed them two or more levels below grade. After 20 weeks of exercises with a variety of texts, only 2 subjects were below. Teachers reported improved reading in the content areas.

Gates and Van Alstyne (1924), working with third through sixth graders (no *N* specified), established two experimental groups and one control group at each grade level. The control group was given no specific practice work; one experimental group had 10 minutes of daily training in reading paragraphs rapidly for important facts, while the other group was trained to read rapidly, followed by discussion in a variety of formats. The mean number of practice periods for both experimental groups was 12.25. All subjects kept track of their scores and were encouraged to improve. The paragraph reading group did better on standardized tests of comprehension than either of the other groups.

In an effort to help improve the comprehension of verbal problems in arithmetic, Greene (1925) had an experimental group of 62 sixth graders work on exercises 10 minutes a day for eight days. The control group of 30 apparently went on with their regular work. Results on the Monroe Standarized Reasoning Test in Arithmetic seemed to favor the experimental group, but the reporting was hazy.

In 1926, Carroll constructed a test on the comprehension of directions and, for a semester, had 30 seventh graders drill with items similar to those on his test. His experimental group outdid the control group in this study and in two additional experiments involving seventh and eighth graders. In the same year, Miles reported on drill work with 331 subjects in grades 9 through 11 paired in control (doing traditional work) and experimental group classes. After 12 weeks of drill on skills selected by each individual experimental class teacher, findings were inconsistent.

Yoakam and Trudy (1926) established an experimental group of 24 fifth grade subjects who worked over a two month period drilling on the telling of what sentences say, selecting the main thought, and selecting the most essential sentences. On the Monroe Silent Reading Test, the experimental class median rose from 4.6 to 8.2; the matched control group median remained at 4.1.

Simpson (1929), concerned with the reading of historical materials, established several experimental groups to compare the merits of answering questions versus evaluating versus outlining versus summarizing. Thirty-five minute periods of from 8 to 32 recitations, dependent upon the school, were scheduled for paired groups of 606 fifth, sixth, and seventh graders. Results on the Thorndike-McCall, the Van Wagenen American History Test, and informal measures showed significant differences in favor of all experimental groups when compared with control groups. Outlining, followed by answering questions about the text, seemed the most effective; summarizing appeared to be least effective. Pupils' ability to retain facts was not enhanced, but they seemed more involved and better able to organize ideas.

McCarty (1931) administered the Thorndike-McCall to 17 ninth and tenth graders six times over a 48 hour period of drill on items like those on that test as well as additional skills. Scores on the Iowa were better, but not significantly so, for the group as compared with a paired control group.

McCallister and Baker (1932) devised units of work on a group of skills for 43 retarded readers in seventh grade English who completed the work in 48 periods of instruction. On the basis of the cumulative scores on the McCall-Crabbs exercises and on the Traxler High School Reading Exercise for Grades VII-IX, the investigators reported that 34 of the 43 made significant gains.

French (1933) had 703 seventh graders work on skill units related to geography. Three weeks each were devoted to vocabulary; organization; and reading maps, graphs, and tables. The researcher found the mean gains of the experimental group were significantly higher than those of a small control group on each unit. Unit tests had been validated and tested for reliability.

Lamoreaux et al. (1934) reported on 4½ months of work with sixth graders (no *N* stated) by three sixth grade teachers to improve reading in content areas–one teacher worked with social studies, one with science, and one with math. Work centered on a variety of skills, and subjects were encouraged to improve and read widely. In each class the greatest gains were made by the lowest and highest groups. The median gain on the Iowa was 15 months in all.

Miller (1934), who endeavored to improve the ability of ninth and twelfth graders to study literature–short prose and poetry selections–through drill on organizing and summarizing, concluded (based on informal test data over one semester) that the average and poor students received the most benefit. Mills and Eckert (1934), who worked with 570 eleventh graders for six weeks, found no effect on comprehension on the Nelson-Denny. Their work consisted of analysis of study methods, lectures on study methods, and the administration of a series of comprehension drills.

Deal (1934) taught three semesters of college students (91, 92, and 87 respectively) to find main ideas, to take notes, and to look up vocabulary words. Emphasis, however, was on drill in rate and comprehension with exercises based on the students' texts. Sixty-four students remained for the second semester and 6 stayed for the third. Control students were given the initial and final drill tests. Experimental students surpassed the control students, although the statistical reporting was unclear.

Gatto (1934) subjected 764 seventh through ninth graders (697 seventh) to teacher-created, factual lessons; classes were held between one and five times a week. Subjects completed an average of five and one-half to eight and one-third lessons; the average gain on the New Stanford was about a year.

In 1936, Walcott conducted one of the few studies in the literature with dull-normal students. He worked with a total of 12 eighth graders and 25 ninth graders in two experiments. Emphasis was placed on worksheets; gains were minor.

McCullough (1937) used units of contemporary materials in addition to encouraging independent reading with 24 ninth graders. After nine weeks of work, there was significant improvement on the Traxler (from just below seventh grade level to just below ninth) and greater gains on the New Stanford. The number of books read appeared to have no relationship to gain. Interestingly enough, the 6 girls in the group showed no significant improvement.

Swenby and Zielsdorf (1951) seemed to "teach" 60 tenth graders, in their English classes, the usual skills using books, magazines, and newspapers. Teachers of world history and biology also tried to emphasize the skills. The mean grade equivalent on the Iowa rose from 7.3 in September to 9.55 in May. The median intelligence quotient on the California Test of Mental Maturity moved from 96 to 101. Without a consideration for standard error or the notion that the intelligence test might reflect reading ability, Swenby and Zielsdorf concluded that many youngsters had been branded stupid when instead "they have missed out in the proper development of reading skills" (p. 357).

Bennett (1953) had three groups of freshmen in college English (no *N* stated) use three separate approaches during a semester: (1) analysis, interpretation, and judgment of reading through writing summary sentences of each paragraph, outlining selections, and/or précis writing; (2) the same as (1) plus additional skill practice and a daily reading exercise; and (3) free reading accompanied by outlining and written analyses. On the Diagnostic, the "extra" skill group scored best in everything except vocabulary. The free reading group scored lowest in everything except speed.

The Ninth Year Committee for the Walton High Schools (1957) reported that, after a full year of work with about 300 female ninth graders on skills related to improving writing and reading in English, general science, and social studies, only 57 students remained below ninth grade level on the Nelson Reading Test as compared with 176 at the outset of the study. Reading skill units had been based on practical English, magazine articles, and various leaflets.

Raygor and Wark (1962) had 56 college students work on programmed materials for two class sessions; one group of 28 used the materials in the normal programmed instruction condition, while the other group used the same materials without reinforcement or feedback. The two groups were compared with 28 random cases who had received the more traditional treatment in the past. Comprehension scores on the Diagnostic showed that both treatments differed significantly from the control but not between themselves. Raygor and Summers (1963) found no significant differences in scores on the Diagnostic after two experiments of three class hours each in which programmed instruction was compared with independent use of the SRA Lab. The first experiment was with eleventh graders and the second with college students.

Ripple (1963) placed 60 college students in each of four conditions (a total of 240): (1) normal programmed instruction; (2) programmed instruction without reinforcement or feedback; (3) conventional reading of programmed material; and (4) conventional lecture based on material. Treatments were administered during a single 50 minute period with no significant difference between programmed conditions (1) and (2). Those in either programmed condition, however, did significantly better than those in the other two conditions, immediately after the treatment or 10 days later.

Livingston (1965) set up three experimental and three control groups of tenth graders (no *N* stated). Three English teachers taught one control and one experimental group two periods a week for five weeks. The teachers selected what they considered appropriate principles and techniques. On the Watson-Glaser Critical Thinking Appraisal, there was a significant difference in the direction of the experimental groups. The study was hindered by teachers' attempting to cope with both experimental and control and with the uncontrolled treatment.

Coulter (1965) investigated the effect of 20 weeks of special instruction in arithmetic training skills on subjects in fourth, fifth, and sixth grades. The reading skills stressed solving word problems, many without quantitative solutions. One group received teacher-directed activities, the other self-study activities. No significant differences in performance were found on the Reading-Arithmetic-Skills Program Test.

Williams and Stevens (1972) studied the effectiveness of teaching third to tenth graders methods for identifying the main ideas of paragraphs. They gave students exercises in underlining topic sentences and writing appropriate titles for graded workbook paragraphs. Secondary students were better able to identify main ideas than elementary students. The investigators felt the results pointed toward a few possibilities—either the skill of finding main idea is developmental, or more real instruction is necessary. Glover et al. (1980) reported that feedback following underlining increased comprehension and produced more "correct" responses (those that matched the researchers') following feedback and, therefore, it might be concluded that underlining alone will not facilitate improved comprehension.

Lowerre and Scandura (1974) developed teaching materials involving two logical inference rules to be used with third and fourth graders. Those in the experimental group received instruction twice a week over a two month period; no instruction was given to the control group. Performance on researcher-created test items favored the experimental group and supported the belief that logical reasoning can be improved using printed material for elementary school subjects reading at the third and fourth grade levels.

Froese and Kurushima (1979) also assessed the effects of sentence expansion practice on third graders' comprehension of passages written at varying levels of syntactic complexity. After training in sentence expansion techniques, the experimental group achieved higher comprehension on passages written at and above their productive level.

Group 2: Drill in Test Taking

Gates (1923) used the Burgess and the Thorndike-McCall tests as drill for third through sixth graders (no *N* stated). Different forms of the tests were given over seven days. "Very slow readers," with the exception of grade three, made marked improvement on the Burgess (emphasis on rate) but not on the Thorndike-McCall (emphasis on comprehension). Gates concluded that an increase in power of comprehension might really depend on growth of native ability over time or upon knowledge and experience.

Dransfield (1925) administered the Thorndike-McCall monthly and informal tests weekly to subjects (no *N* given) across grades 3 through 6. Objectives and scores were posted in classrooms and corridors, and subjects graphed their own scores. For the experimental group, the Thorndike-McCall mean rose from 37.95 to 49.33 from September to May; the control group moved from 40.00 to 47.87.

Group 3: Commercial Materials

A number of researchers used the McCall-Crabbs Test Lessons in Reading series as drill materials. Crofoot (1927) used McCall-Crabbs plus studies of vocabulary, sentences, and paragraphs with 29 experienced teachers in a summer course in remedial reading methods. Farbish (1933) used them with ninth grade boys (*N* not stated) for a "few" months. Limb and Parker (1932) used the materials with 371 children in grades 3 through 7 over a six month period. Crofoot and Farbish reported excellent progress on standardized tests; Limb and Parker found no significant differences between control and experimental groups on median scores in the McCall-Crabbs material.

Burks and Stone (1929), with 404 fourth and fifth graders over a three month period, and Roberts and Stone (1929), with 1,200 fourth and fifth graders over a year, compared McCall-

Crabbs with other drill materials. Subjects did as well with other materials as with McCall-Crabbs when assessed on the Stanford Achievement Test paragraph meaning subtest.

Jacobson and Van Dusen (1930), who combined drill on McCall-Crabbs with Horn's Learn to Study Readers, reported on their work with 150 ninth graders over a 24 week period. The median on the Iowa, for all except high scorers who had been above grade level to begin with, rose from 7.2 to 9.2.

In 1931, Eurich, using a total of 166 experimental and 156 control college students in two experiments, and Thompson (1931), using 38 college students, found no significant gains through drill work as assessed by the Minnesota Reading Examination and the Whipple Silent Reading Test for College Students, respectively.

Jacobson (1933) was interested in learning whether training in reading comprehension transferred to standardized reading tests and to several measures of general science achievement. In the first of two experiments, he subjected 61 experimental and 61 control ninth graders to the same teaching during the first 36 minutes of English class. For the latter 24 minutes of the period, for 12 weeks, control subjects continued in the regular English curriculum, while experimental subjects had 47 intact lessons from readers, 2 from eighth grade history books, and 60 from McCall-Crabbs. Gains were significantly better for the experimental group on the Thorndike-McCall but not in general science. Because of inconsistent findings, Jacobson experimented again with 111 experimental and 95 control subjects in grade 9. The experimental subjects were given 60 exercises using their regular general science texts, while the control subjects carried on their normal study and recitation periods. The experimental group did significantly better on the Gates and the Iowa and on every measure in general science. This last finding convinced Jacobson that giving instruction in reading comprehension in a specific content area was superior to expecting transfer from another content area.

Persons (1934) attempted to improve comprehension in the content areas over a three week period with 953 ninth graders. English teachers tried to develop their students' abilities to summarize, evaluate, and become sensitive to syntax. Prereading activities centered on developing a broad background for the reading and familiarity with patterns and conventions of written discourse. On the New Stanford, 58 percent scored below grade nine at the start; 41 percent scored below after two months of work.

Traxler (1935) had an inexperienced English teacher work with 8 seventh graders in a corrective, pullout program (supervised by the school psychologist). After 23 sessions, subjects showed gains from one-half year to two years on standardized tests administered after the treatment and three months later.

Gray (1936) reported on an incomplete study of 23 college freshmen who met daily in either a rate or a comprehension group. The comprehension group worked on exercises; both groups had weekly meetings on study habits and held individual conferences.

In 1937, Center and Persons established a "reading school" within a large junior-senior city high school. They worked on units of contemporary materials from several content areas for one to three terms with 404 students who scored one or more years below grade level on the New Stanford. An average gain was about 1.4 years in reading, but there was no impact on general scholarship.

Barry and Pratt (1937) and Nutterville and Bloom (1940) worked with high school students who were one year or more below class level. Students in both studies were encouraged to do wide reading, but the main treatment was drill. Barry and Pratt worked with 45 to 78 students who took different tests at different times. They reported 90 percent improvement. Nutterville and Bloom reported that 26 of their 75 ninth graders were at 9.0 or above at the beginning of the semester, while 58 were above at the end of the semester.

According to a Report on Remedial Reading (1939), 13 senior high schools with 3,770 students worked for almost a year on reading units similar to those used by Center and Persons plus a variety of exercise materials. Students gained about one and one-quarter years on a variety of standardized tests at the end of one to four terms.

Johnston, Coleman, and Guiler (1941) grouped 17 fifth graders in an experimental group and 17 in a control group. The experimental group worked over a period of 18 weeks with 35 short reading units accompanied by skill exercises. The experimental group made more progress in reading for facts but not in paragraph comprehension. In the same year (1941), Guiler and Coleman developed exercises for 53 college freshmen. After 22 hours of work, there was an average gain on the Iowa of over three grades, with greatest gains in reading for details and vocabulary.

For 24 weeks, Courigan's (1942) 29 high school subjects read *Reader's Digest* articles and completed accompanying exercises. There was a significant difference on standardized tests of history and literature in favor of the experimental subjects as compared with 29 matched controls. Meade (1948) reported an average gain of 1.4 years on the Iowa by 139 eighth graders after five months of drill on reading skills.

Willey and Thomson (1956) grouped 96 college freshmen into a matched control and experimental group. The experimental group, which worked for a semester on a variety of drill and exercise materials, did significantly better on the Iowa and obtained higher grade point averages after a semester.

Jones and Van Why (1961), Walker (1961), and Rose (1964) used SRA labs with the major intent of improving vocabulary and comprehension. After five months of instruction with 104 fourth graders, Jones and Van Why reported no significant differences on the Iowa Tests of Basic Skills. Walker, who worked with an experimental group of seventh graders on a variety of materials to meet individual needs and a control group of 34 who used the prescribed activities in the SRA Lab, found no significant differences on the Diagnostic Reading test after six weeks of work, 45 minutes daily. Rose, who had volunteer college students work with the SRA Lab over three semesters (some of them remained over three semesters), noted significant improvement on the Diagnostic for the first and third semesters.

Maddison and Rimmington (1966) compared gains in reading achievement for two matched groups after five months of instruction. The control group received traditional instruction; experimentals used the McCall-Crabbs Test Lessons. Those in the experimental group made greater gains on both the California Reading Achievement Test and on lessons in the McCall-Crabbs materials.

Kendrick (1966) reported the basal reader instructional approach superior in effectiveness to the Language Experience Approach. In the LEA group, the students shared ideas through words and pictures, developed writing vocabularies, and wrote stories individually. In the basal approach, chart stories were made from the basal vocabulary and trade books, along with an enrichment series accompanying the basal.

Teacher-Directed Skill Lessons

Eisenhart (1920) compared reading and reporting on easy books without teacher instruction to having teacher-assigned readings with emphasis on the types of questions on standardized tests, as well as retelling, outlining, stating main points, and criticizing the author's views. Third through eighth graders (no *N* given) worked in two separate groups for two 30 minute periods a week for three months. The investigator reported improvement, through percentages, for both treatments.

Rhodes (1922), whose subjects were third through eighth graders (no *N* stated), had student teachers devise exercises for improving comprehension since the pupils had scored poorly on the Burgess Picture Supplement Scale for Measuring Silent Reading. Third through sixth graders made "substantial" progress from January to June, but seventh and eighth graders made little.

Lessenger (1925) worked for a year with 44 good and 67 poor readers from grades three through eight in an effort to improve what he considered to be their faulty reading on the arithmetic subtest of the Stanford Achievement Test. Subjects learned to note and understand key words and technical signs, to see combinations in one eye pulse, and to read important parts unhurriedly without reference to arithmetic. According to the investigator, by the end of the year, 60 percent of the poor and good readers seemed practically free from the faulty habits.

In 1929, Rhoades, as a shift away from drill, focused on larger units of text. He gave 30 superior seventh graders in an experimental group specific training in context clues and finding central ideas of paragraphs in their regular literature books. A control group of 30 read any worthwhile books, discussed them in a variety of ways, and were encouraged to read. The experimental group made the greatest gains on the Stanford.

Keener (1929), with 42 high school students, had teachers spend 15 minutes per day for a semester teaching a number of skills. The semester began with concentration on easy materials, and then students graduated to working with actual texts in science, history, and civics. A control group went on with its regular work in English class. On the Van Wagenen Reading Scale, General Science, experimental subjects showed a gain of two years compared with one year for the control subjects.

Gumlick and Allphin (1931) developed lessons that focused on interpretive abilities for 126 retained third graders and 178 retained fourth graders. The study lasted eight weeks, but little information was given about procedure. The investigators claimed twice the amount of gain that would be considered significant on the Denver Diagnostic Tests.

In 1933, Monroe and Engelhart established experimental classes from a total of 320 fifth graders and control classes of 267 in order to try a systematic program of instruction in reading verbal arithmetic problems over the course of a semester. There were no significant differences, perhaps because, as the investigators pointed out, control subjects also worked on verbal problems.

Bennett (1937) initiated a remedial program for 96 fifth, 116 sixth, 103 seventh, and 114 eighth graders. Subjects were given lessons in comprehension, organization, remembering, and locating information from a variety of texts. On the Iowa, fifth graders gained 2 years; sixth, 19 months; seventh, 21 months; and eighth, 12 months. Details of the lessons were turned into a bulletin to share with other teachers.

McCallister (1942) had 96 junior college freshmen work on a host of study skill activities with emphasis on the higher thought processes. He compared their progress, over 10 to 12 weeks, with 96 who needed such work but did not enter the program. Based on comparisons of scores and percentages on exercises, the investigator concluded that 70 of the 96 improved from one-half to three and one-half years. He felt they gained more than those who had not been trained.

Sayre (1940) and Rudolf (1949), reporting on reading in social studies, demonstrated significant gains for their respective samples on standardized tests after treatment. Sayre had 1,148 seventh through twelfth graders guided through the completion of current event skill exercises one period a week for three months, and 28 of 40 classes made gains greater than could be normally expected on the Master Achievement Tests and the Iowa Silent Reading Test. Rudolf's experimental group of 165 eighth graders received emphasis on "how to read it" skills and on comprehension and study skills while following the regular curriculum. At the end of the semester, the experimental group made significant gains in social studies knowledge, study skills, and reading comprehension as measured by several standardized tests; the control group showed losses in comprehension and study skills.

Ramsey (1957) criticized the laboratory approach to reading improvement and supported teaching reading in the specific content areas. He helped five teachers set up reading programs in eleventh grade English classes. The 425 students studied literature and reading (with emphasis on the Directed Reading Approach) two hours per week for what appeared to be a full school year. Outside reading was encouraged. Scores were reported for only 138 subjects, 78 matched with a control group in a nearby school. On the Cooperative and Diagnostic Reading Tests, improvement was significant in comprehension for the 138; there were significant differences in favor of the experimental group when compared with the control group.

Hislop (1961) established a control and experimental group with 28 division two subjects (grades 4, 5, and 6 in Canada), each group with 14 who scored high and 14 who scored low on the STEP reading test. Experimental subjects were subjected to intensive training in problem solving for a semester with the goal of assessing the effect on both social studies and other reading problems. No significant differences resulted overall; however, the experimental high achievers were superior to the control high achievers in verbalized responses to problems from the STEP social studies test, as well as to social studies problems without guided questions.

The addition of folklore to a program produced a significant increase in the reading achievement of second graders (Sallee, 1983; Sallee & Sethi, 1984). Callaway, McDaniel, and Mason (1972) investigated the effectiveness for first graders of coordinated instruction of oral and written language activities with basal reader instruction. Significantly greater reading comprehension on a standardized reading test was related to spelling basal reader vocabulary words and the writing of compositions unrelated to the basal. Despite inconsistencies, the researchers concluded that a coordinated language arts approach was supported by the data. In a similar investigation of third graders, Smith, Slate, and Morelock (1981) found no significant differences on the Comprehensive Test of Basic Skills between the group receiving an integrated language arts program and those receiving the traditional program in which spelling, language, and reading were treated as distinct subjects.

Vacca (1980) studied the effects of holistic and subskill approaches on the reading comprehension of seventh through ninth graders in a corrective program. The holistic approach included four strategies—uninterrupted SSR; ReQuest, a reciprocal question approach between students and teacher; Radio Reading, a purposeful audience centered oral reading approach; and a DRTA. Subskill instruction centered around eight comprehension subskills. Neither comprehension approach was shown to be superior when achievement test scores were analyzed.

Joseph (1984) reported that academically underprepared college students enrolled in an integrated language skills program performed significantly better on both their final examination and on the Nelson-Denny Reading Test. In a reading program designed to meet the needs of special admit students, Swalm and Cox (1972) developed a procedure of active teaching. Techniques included discussing the main ideas and supporting details of a passage, diagramming the development of its major themes, noting the similarities and differences of ideas in two selections, and transferring the skills to other reading matter. Results obtained on standardized testing showed that the students in the slowest and those in the advanced strands of the program improved significantly.

Working with college freshmen, Draheim (1984) set out to determine the combined effect of the DRTA and conceptual mapping as organizational strategies during the reading of expository texts. Those receiving nine 50 minute sessions over a five week period recalled significantly more main ideas in a summary/analysis task.

Taylor (1986) provided sixth graders with instruction in how to generate main idea statements during six one hour lessons spread out over six weeks. Posttests provided limited support for the notion that it is more useful to instruct students in reading for main ideas in social studies by teaching them how to generate main ideas for social studies passages than by teaching them how to select main idea statements from choices.

Ankney and McClurg (1981) tested the effectiveness of the Guided Reading Procedure (GRP) in aiding the retention of information in texts. Fifth and sixth graders in two social studies classes and two science classes received either the GRP or the usual approach to content reading assignments. Immediately after content was taught using either procedure, pupils took a 10 item multiple-choice test. In a second phase, the control and experimental groups were switched and the procedures repeated. In both phases, the experimental group did better.

In a similar study involving fifth graders in a social studies class, Adams, Carnine, and Gersten (1982) evaluated the effectiveness of explicit systematic instruction as opposed to independent study with feedback or no instruction. Following training in either procedure, subjects were given immediate and delayed posttests, which included retelling the social studies passage and answering a short answer test. The systematic instruction was significantly more effective on short answer tests, but there were no significant differences among groups on the retelling.

Marshall (1984) studied the relative value of the DRTA and the DRA in promoting comprehension as assessed by long-term memory for story content among fourth and fifth graders. The DRA subjects were taught a complete lesson with prereading instruction on appropriate vocabulary, guided reading, and follow-up questions to check comprehension. The DRTA groups were taught a complete lesson with the addition of a follow-up activity in which individual subjects explained how they came up with their predictions. One week after each lesson, individual subjects gave a verbal retelling of the story. The recalls were scored for completeness using the Retelling Checklist, which allowed the quantification of the retellings according to the story elements each contained and the ease of recall for each element. Pupils taught with the DRTA remembered more of the story after the one week delay.

Direct instruction of main idea comprehension proved effective with sixth graders, as reported by Baumann (1984). In contrast with groups receiving either lessons on main idea in a basal series or unrelated vocabulary exercises, the strategy group received intensive main idea instruction according to a paradigm developed by the researcher. They outperformed others in their ability to recognize paragraph main ideas, recognize details that support the main idea, recognize passage main ideas, and compose main idea outlines. The basal group outperformed only on the ability to recognize explicit main ideas. Sjostrom and Hare (1984) described a study in which ninth and tenth graders were afforded main idea lessons in a sequence identifying topics of paragraphs, explicit and implicit main ideas in paragraphs, and main ideas in passages. The control group received instruction in vocabulary development. Those receiving main idea instruction did significantly better on a 13 item production test of main idea identification (researcher devised), summarization of a passage, and the comprehension subtest of the Davis Reading Test.

Gersten and Carnine (1986) offered results of experimental studies supporting explicit, step-by-step training for helping intermediate and secondary students improve reading comprehension. They included studies focusing on teaching students a specific procedure or strategy designed to foster the ability to draw inferences, to increase knowledge of story grammar, and to develop the ability to detect faulty arguments. With gradual withdrawal of teacher guidance, students made significant improvements in targeted comprehension areas.

Austin (1982) conducted a study to determine the effects of study guides on content retention and on reading achievement. The control group received their regular classroom instruction in history class; the experimental group received the same class instruction and, in addition, completed a two page study guide for each of the chapters in the text. Study guides consisted of vocabulary development activities, questions for discussion, statements for acceptance or rejection, and student questions. A test of course content revealed a significant difference favoring the experimental group.

Patchin et al. (1983) studied a direct instruction approach versus a workbook with corrective feedback in training from critical reading skills. After the three day instructional intervention had been completed, fifth graders were given a specially designed critical reading test of 15 passages designed to assess whether they could detect valid or invalid instances of an argument. Results favored the systematic instruction approach over the workbook. Kennon and Noland (1983) found the Cognitive Development Approach to Moral Education successful in improving the inferential comprehension skills of sixth graders. The approach consisted primarily of reading two novels, followed by a discussion of the moral dilemmas found in the novels.

Readence, Baldwin, and Head (1987) reported that third graders did significantly better on a test of metaphors after receiving a three day instructional procedure designed to teach a process for interpreting metaphors than did their counterparts in the control group, who received metaphor instruction found in a basal series.

Rereading

Yoakam (1921) had 417 subjects in grades 4 through 8 read factual selections of varying lengths from textbooks. There were no time constraints, but subjects read only once and then were tested on comprehension. Overall comprehension was poor, but better retention was evident when a test of prior knowledge was administered in advance of the reading. Yoakam suggested that future researchers investigate the efficiency of various rereadings and repeated testing. He concluded that "the motivation due to the initial test and the effect of the repetition of the tests apparently far outweigh in importance the brief, though indispensable, contact with the material" (p. 101).

With a large number of subjects from fifth through ninth grades and college, Germane (1920, 1921a, 1921b, 1921c, 1921d) explored the effects of rereading on comprehension compared with summarizing. When his concept of summarizing included specific questions raised in advance of the reading to be answered mentally after one reading, followed by skimming for unrecalled answers, the summarizing groups did better than the reread groups on a "rigorous" test. When summarizing groups were asked to write main points in an article, the rereading alone groups did better on the tests of immediate and delayed recall. Germane issued a cry, however, for spending more time on teaching comprehension since even the rereading groups' median scores were very low. He also felt that raising questions before reading was a valuable tool for increasing comprehension.

Arnold (1942) compared four study techniques in the field of history with 114 college freshmen and 124 sophomores as subjects. Four groups were carefully equated, and techniques were rotated among the groups. Techniques were: repetitive reading alone, underlining and marginal notes, outlining, and précis writing or brief summarizing. The study began with three weeks of concentration on drill work, homework, and proficiency tests for all subjects. A questionnaire was used to test preknowledge, and the topic of Latin America was selected since subjects seemed to know least about it. Then each of the four groups studied separate bodies of information over 12 weekly study sessions, with each concentrating on a different technique. The results on an objective test given immediately and five weeks later showed no significant differences, although there was a trend in the direction of underlining or reading alone for immediate recall.

Good (1926) worked with college and high school subjects (no *N* stated) to determine the effect on comprehension of a single reading versus two readings. Results were inconsistent, and analysis was limited to "eyeballing." Crawford (1929) pitted one reading against two readings against outlining with 346 college students. There were no significant differences among the treatments, although any training showed significant improvement over a group that had not been involved in the study.

Mathews (1938) placed 735 students in 10 high schools in three roughly equivalent groups to learn whether reading alone without notes, underlining, or taking outline notes was the most effective study method. Test results for immediate recall and organization were superior for the group that read alone without taking notes. Testing one month later showed that the ninth and tenth graders did best after taking outline notes, but eleventh and twelfth graders still did best with reading alone. Stordahl and Christensen (1956) tested four conditions (rereading, underlining, summarizing, and outlining) with 200 Air Force trainees, 50 placed randomly in each cell. Each subject studied for an hour. Treatments had no differential effect on test scores for immediate or delayed recall.

In 1964, Hill tested the influence of prereading directions on comprehension and rate, as well as the influence of rereading on comprehension, with 54 English education majors. Subjects read three selections, each with a different prereading condition. Five days later, by random selection, 37 of the subjects reread to correct errors made on the initial test; the subjects felt this strategy was useful and quite unusual in their scholastic experience. There was a significant difference in comprehension following rereading, but no significant difference in prereading conditions.

Hoon (1974) assessed the effectiveness of rereading, reading with underlining, and reading with notetaking on multiple choice comprehension with 30 undergraduate students. Prior to a comprehension test, subjects were given two minutes to review underlinings, notes, or the text itself. There were no significant differences among the study groups. In a similar study, Orlando and Hayward (1978) found notetaking and mental reviewing to be superior to rereading with college students. Dyer, Riley, and Yekovich (1979) found notetaking and rereading to be superior to summarizing for both undergraduate and graduate students.

Rashotte and Torgesen (1985) studied whether a procedure of repeated readings was more effective than an equal amount of nonrepetitive reading and whether the degree of word overlap among passages affects comprehension and fluency in repeated readings. Learning disabled pupils, ages 8.6 to 12, were asked to read a number of passages using three treatments: (1) repeated reading in which the number of words shared among stories was low and relatedness of content was minimal, (2) repeated reading in which the word overlap among passages was high, and (3) reading of passages similar to the second condition but with each passage being read only once. Treatments lasted 15 minutes daily for seven days and included four passage presentations with four comprehension questions following the first reading and one comprehension question after each remaining reading. No significant differences were noted for comprehension.

O'Shea, Sindelar, and O'Shea (1985) considered the effect of attentional cues in addition to repeated readings. Subjects were assigned to one of two treatments: a cue to read quickly and accurately, and a cue to read for comprehension. Both fluency and comprehension increased as the number of readings increased. Pupils who were cued to read quickly and accurately had a higher mean number of words read correctly per minute but a lower number of propositions retold than those who were cued to read for comprehension.

Reading Practice

Stone and Colvin (1920) introduced a procedure wherein students would be encouraged to reflect on their own reading and study before engaging in these processes. Prior to beginning study, 45 college juniors in an educational psychology class discussed factors important in study and made a list on which they rated themselves. After 20 hours of reading individual, relatively easy books and 10 hours of reading more difficult material in a single textbook, the subjects rated themselves again. They improved on a test (undescribed) by "more than half."

Stone (1922) generated, over a semester, two experimental and two control groups from 15 college classes of juniors, seniors, and graduate students at two universities. He set up one practice group of 142 subjects who practiced reading in material related to a given course, and a partial practice group of 130 who paid no particular attention to reading as such but took many tests and had extensive assignments in collateral reading. The researcher reported "notable" results on the Monroe with a range of 36 percent to 74 percent gains for practice groups, 37 percent to 44 percent for partial practice groups, and 21 percent for the controls who had no special tests or reading assignments.

In 1927, over a four week period, Good studied the extensive versus the intensive reading of three pairs of parallel college students (30 to 50 in each of the paired groups). No clear superiority of one type of reading over the other was ascertained.

Wagner (1932) subjected 54 high school juniors to six sessions of rapid reading with the goal of improving both rate and comprehension. Six weeks after the sessions, she administered the Nelson-Denny to the 54, as well as to untrained groups. The rapid reading group showed a slight superiority in comprehension.

Over the course of a semester, Goldberg (1946) compared wide reading to intensive drill, using two high school remedial classes and one control group. Nelson-Denny scores on 18 matched subjects showed that the controls were much higher in vocabulary, but did not do well in paragraph comprehension. The extensive reading group surpassed the drill group in paragraph comprehension.

Oliver (1973) compared sixth graders who were allowed to spend 30 minutes a day involved in SSR instead of the traditional directed reading program offered to the control group. Gains on the Gates-MacGinitie Reading Test favored those involved in SSR, but the gains were not significant. Wolf and Mikulecky (1978) studied the effects of skills instruction alone and skills instruction plus SSR on seventh graders. No significant differences were found on vocabulary between the two groups. A mean score decline was found for comprehension by the SSR group.

Hicks (1983) evaluated the effects of SSR as a supplement to a regular basal program in a sixth grade class. Pupils showed growth on the Stanford Achievement Test at the end of the school year. Kefford (1981) described a reading scheme in which one English period per week was used in a library based SSR time. Subjects read novels chosen from thematically organized lists. After the first six months, subjects showed improvement in vocabulary and comprehension.

Farrell (1982) studied junior high school students engaged in SSR combined with discussion and writing about their reading. Ninety percent of the subjects improved between one and two years on the Gates-MacGinitie Reading Test. Manning and Manning (1983) reported that pupils involved in SSR as a recreational activity showed gains in reading achievement when the procedure was coupled with peer interaction concerning their reading.

Rehder (1980) investigated amount of reading, attitude toward reading, and reading achievement scores for high school juniors and seniors enrolled in a popular fiction class using high interest paperbacks. Students were required to read a minimum of nine books over 18 weeks, to complete one or more assignments for each book, and to pass an objective test on the book. In addition to showing a gain on standardized testing, growth in enjoyment of reading also occurred. Similarly, when eighth graders were given magazines that appealed to their interests, reading scores improved significantly (Rucker, 1982).

Study Skills

Beauchamp (1923) set out to determine the value of a set of procedures on mastery of elementary physical science subject matter. Over a six month period, he worked with 26 eighth graders and established a control group with 26 others. He observed process and assessed product through informal tests in both comprehension and speed. During the first five weeks, both groups were subjected to carefully designed subject matter lessons. Both groups continued such lessons for the rest of the time, but the experimental group had skills and strategies added. First, deciding on central ideas was added for four weeks, with test scores favoring the experimental group; however, the experimental subjects tended to take notes showing a prominence of major points and how each point related to the whole, used more of their own words, took fewer notes, and seemed to take more time to think and read than to write. Control behaviors appeared to be directly opposite.

Helseth (1926) sought to learn whether emphasis placed on methods of study rather than recitation of facts would make her 7 seventh graders conscious of study methods without causing losses on standardized tests. A student teacher worked with the class for 55 minutes a day over eight months using a single American history text for instruction. Helseth considered her study a process-product approach. One or more observers and the critic teacher took notes that were read by the investigator at the end of the year (process). Standardized tests of American history as well as the Van Wagenen scales (product) showed superiority over the norms for both seventh and eighth graders. Process successes appeared to be reporting accurately from reading, improving research techniques, learning sequential order, organizing conclusions in brief form, noting both sides of a question, organizing main ideas and details clearly, developing insights into study methods, and developing independence in learning.

Witty and Lehman (1927) worked with 80 college students for a regular semester and during the summer and found that reading practice followed by the writing of summaries resulted in improved scores on both the Thorndike-McCall and the Monroe.

Book (1927) conducted two experiments with college students, emphasizing the reading of directions in relevant assignments and how they were followed. They also were given instruction on learning how to read using the investigator's textbook on the subject. In the first experiment, 54 students made 102 percent improvement on the investigator-designed test. In the second experiment, results on the Whipple Test for College Students and the Indiana University Reading Test for 112 subjects were compared with those of other university students. These students had a "percentage of efficiency" rating of 69.5 compared with a rating of 59.2 for the others.

Newlun (1930) divided 276 fifth graders into experimental and control groups; for 12 weeks experimental groups were taught (emphasis seemed mainly on practice) to summarize readings in their history text. High achievers in summarizing did significantly better on the Simpson-Gambrill-Moore Test of History than control subjects, but there were no significant differences on the Sangren-Woody Reading Test.

Moore's (1934) 41 college freshmen showed much improvement on the investigator-designed test after they drilled for six weeks on items similar to those on the test. In addition, weekly 40 minute peer conferences were held in which subjects received help in course work and constructed a weekly study schedule.

Salisbury (1934) asked if training in outlining and summarizing in English class carried over to other content areas and if the skills made a difference in reading comprehension. She established 150 matched pairs of seventh, ninth, and twelfth graders. Experimental subjects studied 30 lessons on outlining and summarizing; control subjects had 30 lessons in material directly from the English curriculum. Experimental lessons were focused on the "thinking side" of outlining, use of topic markers, transition expressions, and converting outlines into summaries. Although not significantly, experimental subjects did better on reasoning and content transfer tests than control subjects. Experimental subjects had significant gains on the Haggerty Reading Test.

Sheldon (1948), who worked with 16 medical school students in 50 minute periods twice a week for nine weeks, had them read popular magazines, discuss aspects of reading, and then read in their texts. Work on a tachistoscope also was provided. At the beginning of the study, only 3 students achieved fiftieth percentile ranking on the Iowa; at the close, only 2 did not.

Several researchers tested the effectiveness of SQ3R or questioned its success in comparison with other techniques. Donald (1967) compared reading, history, and geography achievement of seventh graders after using the SQ3R method of study. The experimental group was taught the method in social studies classes, while the control group followed a traditional method that included group work, oral and written reports, silent and oral reading of content, and answering questions. No significant differences were reported on the Coordinated Scales of Attainment. Eanet (1978) assessed the efficacy of a reading/study procedure (REAP) for increasing reading achievement with undergraduates in a college reading and study skills class. The six sections of the class were assigned to one of the three treatments: the REAP group, an experimental/control group receiving instruction in SQ3R and related skills practice, and a control group getting instruction in affective readiness for study skills with subsequent instruction and practice in study skills areas not directly related to study reading or comprehension improvement. The control group scored highest on standardized testing.

Shoop (1982) studied the effects of three instructional strategies (cloze, study guide, and a combination method using cloze and study guide) on inferential comprehension of eighth graders. Subjects in the cloze treatment group completed passages from social studies texts in which deletions had been made in a regular pattern. The study guide treatment group answered inferential questions over the same intact passages. The combination group alternated these treatments. Following final instruction, subjects were given a 40 item posttest of multiple-choice inferential questions on which the combination group did significantly better. Researchers indicated that training in the use of multiple context clues through the use of cloze passages enabled subjects to score higher on test items involving the same type of processing (Rankin et al., 1980; Risko & Redelheim, 1981; Sampson, Valmont, & Allen, 1982).

Jacques and Corrin (1981) analyzed the effects of instruction using study guides in critical reading skills for college freshmen. Students in the experimental group showed significant growth in both literal and inferential skills. Jacques (1982) also found that college freshmen scored higher on the Stanford Diagnostic Reading Test and the Watson-Glaser Critical Thinking Appraisal with practice on the skills of recognizing assumptions, reading deductively, interpreting, drawing inferences, and evaluating arguments.

Coles and Foster (1975) reported three related studies comparing comprehension scores of college undergraduates after reading text with or without core sentences underlined. Students' prereading instructions varied from none to directions to use SQ3R. In the first study, the experimental materials—core statements or their equivalents—were underlined and the students were given no special instructions. In the second, students were given written instructions in regard to the underlined points. In the third, the students were exhorted to follow SQ3R procedures and were just informed of the underlining. The results showed no significant differences in the first and second studies. In the third, students given both underlined text and told to use SQ3R had significant gains compared with the group that did not use those procedures. A number of researchers compared underlined text with other procedures such as preview summaries or italicized text (Dunman, 1973; Richmond, 1973; Taub, 1984). There were no significant differences in effects among procedures reported.

Some researchers thought that the more active involvement of underlining text would facilitate greater comprehension. Idstein and Jenkins (1972) studied underlining compared with repetitive reading of college students. No significant differences between study techniques were found. Working with senior high school and junior college students, Schnell and Rocchio (1978) sought to determine if prior reading ability affected the value of underlining techniques. They found no significant differences for ability, but they did report that when students underlined materials or used materials that had been underlined their comprehension was better than that of students who had not incorporated either technique.

Shikanai (1980) investigated the effects of summarizing, notetaking, and underlining with college students in Japan. Although differences were slight, students in the reading and notetaking group gave more examples of the main theme.

Grabe (1980) examined the influence of a highlighting task on the recall of relevant information. Fourth and sixth graders were asked to either read and mark any material they felt to be important or to read and mark the material in the story related to a prescribed topic. After reading, subjects were told to write all they could remember. Better readers recalled more relevant idea units. Fowler and Barker (1974) reported no significant differences when college students were directed to either highlight the text, read the material highlighted by the researchers, or read material highlighted by another group.

Bigler (1984) studied the effectiveness of two direct instruction techniques for increasing skills in drawing conclusions and predicting outcomes. Mildly retarded pupils, ages 9 through 12, were taught either underlining key elements or modeling and practice in thinking aloud. The treatments occurred over six sessions of 15 to 20 minutes each. Inferential questions requiring predictions or conclusions were asked daily, both after reading a story and after listening to a story. Performance improved on a researcher-created Inference Rating Scale, but differences were not significant.

Englert and Lichter (1982) described a program to improve organizational skills of sixth grade learning disabled pupils. Subjects were trained in a "statement-pie" technique consisting of a procedure for seeking two major categories of concepts. The object was to locate the statement, main idea, or topic of the passage that subsumed other related concepts. The reader sought the pie or written proofs, information, and examples that were devoted to support of the statement. Gains in reading comprehension skills on the Peabody Individual Achievement Tests were substantial over those of the previous academic year.

Training in summary writing appeared to be a successful strategy for improving comprehension. King, Biggs, and Lipsky (1984) compared the effects of student-generated prequestions and summaries as reading/study strategies. College students were trained to use one of the two study approaches: phrasing and answering higher level questions while reading, or constructing and checking summary statements while reading. A control group received no training. Instruction in summary generation as an adjunct study activity significantly increased subjects' free recall as well as performance on objective and essay tests. Training in interspersed prequestions significantly aided students' performance on objective but not on essay tests. The researchers concluded that college students benefitted more from engaging in encoding strategies during reading.

Cunningham (1982) studied the effectiveness of teaching the writing of summary sentences for paragraphs. Graduate students were taught to write gist statements for paragraphs and subsequently did better on a simplified text analysis procedure testing their ability to get the major points. Hare and Borchardt (1984) conducted one of the few studies wherein one might accurately state the effect of training in a procedure. Not only were these researchers examining the effect of teaching summary writing to high school juniors, but they used summaries written by subjects for pre and postinstructional data. Those receiving summarization training did significantly better than those without training. In a similar study conducted with fifth graders, McNeil and Donant (1982) found that training in the rules of summary writing allowed all subjects to do better on comprehension questions and produce better written summaries.

Bean and Steenwyk (1984) delivered three types of summarization instruction to sixth graders. The two treatment groups received either a rule-governed approach or an intuitive approach. Controls simply received advice to find the main ideas with no explicit modeling. Treatment groups significantly outperformed the control group on both a paragraph summary writing task and the Nelson Reading Test of paragraph comprehension.

Rinehart, Stahl, and Erickson (1986) offered a summarization training program to sixth graders to improve their reading and study skills. Training improved recall of major but not minor information on the study tasks. The training also improved summaries of paragraphs with main ideas stated, but not those in which the statement of main idea had to be invented.

Hayes and Readence (1982) studied the effect of illustrating text concerned with spatial relations. Subjects worked through the texts and completed the exercises under four conditions: text without illustrations, line drawings, line drawings with subjects instructed to attend to the illustrations, and no illustrations and subjects told to imagine their own pictures to go along with texts. Subjects performed better on the study exercises when illustrations were given. Hayes and Readence (1983) reported similar results in the transfer of learning from illustration-dependent text. Additional 150 word transfer passages were given for each text based on concepts in the main text. After each presentation, subjects were asked to recall, in writing, the transfer texts.

Dutton (1978) explored the differences among several methods of teaching three dimensional forms to 11 and 12 year old children. Students were divided into those getting contour maps and models and those getting only two dimensional maps. On a comprehension test, students in the contour maps and models group performed significantly better than their counterparts.

Instrument Presentations

Dearborn and Wilking (1941), who worked with 30 college freshmen for six weeks, developed a manual of college reading focused on history, English, and science. The emphasis was on thoroughness, organizational patterns, and "the reader's participation in what the writer is attempting to express" (p. 672), which they called "associative reading," a concept never really clarified. The gain was significant for level of comprehension on the Cooperative, as well as for vocabulary and total test on the Nelson-Denny.

Westover (1946) compared Strang's Study Type of Reading Exercises with adapted questions to the same material used on the Reading Pacemaker, an instrument that controlled eye movements in phrases. Two experimental groups of 45 college freshmen were compared with a control group of 50. While control subjects went on with their regular college work, experimental subjects worked on the exercises, with or without the instrument, for two 50 minute periods a week for five weeks. The instrument group showed the most significant gains in level of comprehension on standardized tests. Both experimental groups had significantly more students with good scholarship grades and fewer who withdrew from school.

Beasley (1959) used a type of pacer, the SRA Reading Accelerator, with 138 college freshmen. Thirty-six hours were spent on group instruction using a number of reading skill texts; most of the 24 hours of individual work was allotted to work on pacers. Improvement was significant as assessed by the Diagnostic given immediately after and again three months later.

Mayhew and Weaver (1960) set up four conditions with 96 college freshmen, 11 to 13 in a group, for two fall semesters: (1) materials accompanying the Harvard Reading Films (not projected) plus lectures on skills and some individual help; (2) SRA Better Reading Books and Progress folders plus lectures and individual help; (3) both sets of materials as in (1) and (2) plus Harvard Reading Films (projected) and tachistoscopic training; and (4) both sets of materials without instrumentation. No significant differences were found on the comprehension subtest of the California.

Bottomly (1961) divided 460 fifth and eighth graders into experimental and control classes and used the Controlled Reader with experimental classes four times a week in 40 minute lessons for roughly two months. The control group followed an "eclectic" program. No significant differences surfaced at the end of the study on the Cooperative for grade eight or the Chicago Reading Test for grade five. Five months later, however, the Controlled Reader group showed significant differences over the eclectic group.

Martens (1961) matched two groups of 48 high school girls. Twice a week for one semester, both groups spent the first 10 minutes of a 45 minute period completing a rate of comprehension test. The experimental group used individual, mechanical rate pacers, while the control group read the same material in the usual manner. No significant differences emerged on the California at the end of the semester six months later.

Olson, Sanford, and Ohnmacht (1964) used the C-B Educational Films Developmental Reading Program and Phrase Reading Workbooks to teach study techniques every other week for eight 50 minute periods to an experimental group of 145 college freshmen majoring in education. A control group of 174 freshmen girls majoring in liberal arts also was established. At the outset, the control group was superior to the experimental on all subtests of the Nelson-Denny. By the end of the semester, the experimental group gained parity with the control group except for vocabulary.

McDowell (1964) established 16 experimental and 16 control groups of fifth graders who were near, on, or above grade level. The experimental Controlled Reader program was compared with a basal reader program. The treatment for both groups was given for 30 minutes four times a week (total number of sessions unstated). The Gates Reading Inventory showed no significant differences.

Berger (1967) and Braam and Berger (1968) included tachistoscopic, controlled readers, controlled pacers, and paperback scanning in college reading improvement courses. In the first study, no significant gains were found, but in the second study, significant gains were found for all approaches except that using the tachistoscope. With ninth graders, Gelzer and Santore (1968) compared various reading approaches. These included using controlled readers, shadowscopes, and ratemeters. The group receiving controlled reader training had significantly higher scores.

Computer assisted instruction (CAI) provided another means whereby technology was offered as a source for improving reading comprehension. Midgett, Thompson, and Walters (1985) assessed the effectiveness of a CAI reading tutorial program emphasizing vocabulary and reading skills for fifth graders. While the CAI subjects worked with the computer in addition to class instruction, the control group received regular classroom instruction. Comparison of the scores on the Comprehensive Tests of Basic Skills revealed no significant differences between groups. Boettcher (1983) described the design and content of a computer based, commercially prepared reading program containing 240 short passages and presenting five comprehension skills areas for diagnosis and practice. She also presented the results of two studies in which students were instructed with the program; results on the California Achievement Test were mixed.

Word Study

McDonald and Pauk (1956) reported helping 116 college freshmen (equated with a control group of 142) learn to pay attention to what they called "functional vocabulary development" (attention to word derivation and context) while reading sets of related paragraphs. The experimental group exceeded the control (.01) on the Cooperative. Over three semesters, the experimental group showed significant difference when compared with the control group and with the entire freshman class.

In a study focusing on the effect of direct vocabulary instruction on comprehension test scores of middle school students, Tuinman and Brady (1974) developed a series of exercises in which students were given the definitions of the words and then asked to (1) determine if the words were used correctly in example sentences, (2) complete fill-in sentences with an appropriate word, (3) answer open-ended questions in which they had to know the word meanings to complete the activity, and (4) use and illustrate the words. Results on researcher-constructed tests of word knowledge showed scores improving on the vocabulary tests, but there was little if any contribution of increased word knowledge to reading comprehension.

Groebel (1979) compared the use of self-help dictionary study in conjunction with a traditional approach requiring only that college students read and prepare a text for class. Cloze testing to assess reading comprehension revealed no significant differences between groups.

Aulls and Gelbart (1980) investigated the effectiveness of vocabulary training on the reading comprehension of seventh graders. Able readers outperformed less able readers on tests of literal comprehension following a procedure of vocabulary training with guided silent reading by means of a paced reading technique.

Wixson (1986) examined the effects of using two different methods (dictionary or concept) of instruction to preteach vocabulary of basal stories. The results of the dictionary treatment indicated that preteaching unfamiliar vocabulary enhanced children's comprehension of story ideas that were related to the instructed vocabulary. The results of the concept method were unclear because of interactions with the story. Of importance was the suggestion that comprehension questions designed to evaluate students' understanding of story ideas that related to the instructed vocabulary provided a more sensitive measure of children's comprehension than a general recall measure.

Vaughn et al. (1982) considered the effects of preteaching vocabulary on the comprehension of science text material. In the experience-based treatment, vocabulary related to key concepts in the text was taught prior to reading by introducing terms similar to each vocabulary item and discussing similarities and differences. In the definition-based treatment, vocabulary and definitions were introduced via a ditto or chalkboard. In the control group, no vocabulary instruction was given. In response to short answer comprehension questions, subjects in the experience-based group scored significantly higher than the other two groups. In contrast, Stahl (1983) found that a definitional method had a significant effect on comprehension as indicated on a sentence anomaly test, a sentence cloze test, and a multiple-choice test. When the definitional treatment was combined with contextual information, higher comprehension scores were realized than from using the definitional mode alone.

Roser and Juel (1982) studied the extent to which pupils need to learn designated "new" vocabulary words prior to their encounter with the passage. Subjects were taught the words using a technique that included direct teaching, drawing relationships between vocabulary and the readers, and indepth treatment. The lower ability groups showed more significant gains on reading comprehension than those receiving no instruction. Similarly, Carney et al. (1984) found that preteaching vocabulary terms in social studies related to significant gains in both immediate and long term comprehension.

The effect of long term vocabulary instruction on lexical access and reading comprehension was considered by Beck, Perfetti, and McKeown (1982). Words were taught in two frequency conditions: "some," in which 8 to 10 new words were taught and reinforced through daily lessons for five days; and "many," in which subsets of words from the "some" condition reappeared in review cycles. An additional set of words similar in difficulty, length, and semantic similarity was designated as "none" and appeared only on pre and posttests. Subjects showed large gains on the reading subtests of the Iowa Test of Basic Skills. In a replication study, McKeown et al. (1983) included story recall for assessment and found that instruction enhanced knowledge of the instructed words and comprehension of stories containing these words.

The examination of transfer following the training of pupils to decode words more quickly and accurately led to the conclusion that readers would do better on word recognition tests, but their performance on comprehension tests would not be significantly affected (Fleisher, Jenkins, & Pany, 1979; Spring, Blunden, & Gatheral, 1981). Similarly, Cunningham, Cunningham, and Rystrom (1981) found no significant differences in reading comprehension achievement when pupils were offered a syllabication strategy. Wallach and Wallach (1979), however, found that first and second graders benefitted both in word recognition and comprehension from a tutorial emphasizing phoneme identification skills.

Blanchard (1980) studied the transfer of single word decoding training to contextual, literal, and inferential reading comprehension. Below average sixth graders were taught to read all the words used in a passage (content specific) or were taught to read another set of words, none of which appeared in the passage. After learning the words, all subjects read the passages, and their reading comprehension was assessed. The content specific training group answered significantly more literal and inferential questions correctly than did those given noncontent specific training.

A comparison of training in word recognition and comprehension strategies was conducted by Fleisher and Jenkins (1983). Learning disabled fourth and fifth graders were exposed to three different approaches. The first emphasized comprehension—subjects were regularly questioned about reading content and were corrected on oral reading errors. The second approach was word emphasis instruction—pupils were corrected for all reading errors and received error-word drills daily. The third method combined aspects of the two, including word error corrections and drills, along with comprehension questions. No differences were found among treatment effects on comprehension and oral reading; on isolated word recognition measures, the approach that included error-word drills produced higher scores.

Oral Presentations

Cline (1965) used an audiovisual program that concentrated on vocabulary and reading comprehension. Spanish speaking fourth and fifth grade pupils were taught daily in half-hour sessions with the available equipment in the schools. The program used commercially available films, filmstrips, slides, and records. A comparison group was taught without audiovisual support, except for that used by the classroom teacher. After two years, the experimental group made greater gains on standardized testing.

Orr (1968) examined the effectiveness of simultaneous reading and listening with mentally retarded 12 and 17 year olds who had reading grade equivalents of at least 2.0. The treatments consisted of reading the text on film and hearing a recording; reading the text on film and hearing the teacher read orally; and hearing the text on tape played at a reduced rate without visual support. There were no significant differences among methods.

Statistically significant differences favoring training in listening were found in studies conducted by Lemons and Moore (1982) and Lemons and Malatesha (1985). Previously, Cohen (1969) studied the effect of daily listening to literature on the achievement of primary students from low socioeconomic homes. Pupils were taught reading in a prescribed curriculum stressing a basal reading approach. In addition, the subjects in the experimental group listened to selected stories read by their teachers. The instructional program was related to the literature program and stressed examination of the events, concepts, and relationships within the stories. The experimental group showed significantly higher results on the Metropolitan.

Seaton and Wielan (1981) compared the effectiveness of parallel lessons in listening and silent reading with a traditional basal approach for fifth graders. The listening/reading transfer method consisted of two parallel lessons designed by the teacher. The first lesson had subjects listening to a topic and responding in specific ways, and the second followed a similar pattern with silent reading instead of listening. On the New Development Reading Test, the experimental group showed significantly greater gain scores on reading for relationships, reading for interpretation, and reading for appreciation. Boodt (1984) evaluated the effectiveness of a program emphasizing six critical listening skills on critical reading, listening, and thinking abilities. She found that subjects in the experimental group showed significant gains on STEP: Listening and Reading, and A Look at Literature: The NCTE Cooperative Test of Critical Reading and Appreciation.

Wiseman, Hartwell, and Kannafin (1980) assessed the effects of various conditions for acquiring textbook content by mildly handicapped high school students. Probe 1 examined the students' performance in reading a text passage followed by a written response to questions about the passage. Probe 2 compared three instructional formats for presenting textbook content through listening, using recall responses by aural-oral means. Probe 3 duplicated the text presentation of Probe 2, but the response type was altered to require answers to multiple-choice questions. Reading test scores on a standardized test seemed to have little relationship to performance on the textbook assignments for either reading or listening conditions. Results of the probes indicated that listening to text content was generally as effective or more effective than reading textbook content, but on all probes there was a high degree of variability in performance.

Heckelman (1969) used a combination oral reading and listening procedure, the Neurological Impress method, for 15 minutes daily over a period of six weeks. Results as measured on the California Achievement Test showed gains in reading comprehension for 24 remedial reading students in grades 7 through 10.

Lorenz and Vockell (1979) examined the effectiveness of the Neurological Impress method on the comprehension of second through fifth grade learning disabled pupils. The experimental subjects were given the impress method, and the controls received traditional remedial reading techniques. No significant differences were found in comprehension before or after treatment. When Bos (1982) added assisted and repeated readings to the impress method, she found that with this repeated choral reading procedure subjects gained in comprehension.

In a study of culturally different remedial students in upper elementary grades, Laffey, Kelly, and Perry (1980) reported on the effect on reading achievement of repeated readings of taped literature. The experimental group listened to taped stories for about 15 minutes daily for 13 weeks. After listening two to three times, they were encouraged to read along orally until fluency was achieved. No significant differences were reported between groups. In a similar study, Laffey and Kelly (1981) used the same procedures with remedial readers in fifth and sixth grades. When tested on the California Achievement Test, subjects in the treatment group scored significantly higher than the control group on comprehension and total reading.

Abelson and Petersen (1983) studied the effectiveness of the "talking book" on the reading/listening comprehension of reading disabled boys from grades 4, 5, and 6. The talking book was described as a read along cassette tape recording including background music and effects that accompanied reading material. Three different stories were presented using three different methods of presentation: the talking book approach, listening only to a tape of the story, and attempting to read along silently as an adult read aloud. Ten direct recall questions were used to evaluate comprehension; no significant differences in proficiency were detected.

Schema Activation

Specific Preorganizers

Bird (1918) considered her first semester group of 100 college students in a course in educational psychology as a control group and the second semester group of 100 as the experimental group. In the experimental treatment, she helped subjects get ready to read a chapter, "The Nervous System as the Organ of Behavior," in the text by explaining difficult parts of the chapter. This was supplemented by the introduction of a model of the brain and a preserved human brain. The average grade for the experimental group was 74.10 percent, as contrasted to 54.15 percent for the control on a posttest. Bird felt that there was adequate evidence to support careful assignments in the form of supervised study aimed at catching the attention and interest of the students.

Springsteed (1925) helped teachers in 85 fourth through eighth grade classes in which the majority of students came from foreign language homes to mobilize and improve their children's schemata in relation to what was about to be read. Children were questioned about what they read and then asked to write a summary in order to "review the story as a unit." After two months of work, scores on the Chapman-Cook Speed of Reading Test indicated that only 3 of the 50 classes below grade level in speed and comprehension remained below grade level.

Gatto (1927) had seventh graders in an experimental American history class read short, related selections in advance of studying a chapter, while the control group continued the traditional program. In the experimental class, he also raised questions in advance "to enhance the salient points of the material presented and to create a mental set conducive to a more intelligent understanding" (p. 4). The 76 subjects, divided into experimental and control groups, studied 12 lessons in the text over a period of five weeks.

The experimental group exceeded the control group by 25.5 percent on a comprehension posttest designed by the investigator.

E.L. Smith (1973) gave low reading ability community college students instruction in surveying and constructing preoutline organizers from the title, subheadings, and italicized words in texts; developing questions from the organizer; reading to answer the questions; filling in the organizer; and reviewing the completed outline. In comparison with those not receiving the instruction, there were no significant differences in performance on a researcher-made test.

Smith and Hesse (1969) used an orally presented organizer to improve the reading comprehension of secondary school students. They called their technique a cognitive organizer, which contained background information and traced the sequence in which the author presented the content. A posttest to the experimental group and a comparison group (which only read the passage) assessed ability to recall details, make inferences, and select main ideas. The results showed the cognitive organizer had a positive effect on the comprehension of poor readers, but a negative effect on the comprehension of good readers. Bean (1981) explored the degree to which a teacher-guided discussion of major concepts and relationships prior to reading would facilitate comprehension of college students in a reading improvement course. After reading, a 10 item multiple-choice test was given, followed one week later by an alternate form of the test. The overview was found to be generally effective for both levels of readers on short term comprehension but not on long term comprehension.

Andrews (1971, 1972-1973) compared the effects on seventh and eleventh graders' reading comprehension of two types of advance organizers—directed reading questions and cognitive organizers. The directed reading questions were to set a purpose for the assigned reading as an aid to comprehension. They consisted of an example and three alternate possibilities for the passages' main idea. The cognitive organizer provided general information and the sequence of ideas about the assigned reading. Results on a 10 item comprehension test indicated significant differences favoring the cognitive organizer group.

Sachs (1983) randomly assigned learning disabled children to one of three prereading treatments. Students received training in a modified DRA, a modified Concept Analysis Activity, or a Worksheet Activity (control). No significant differences were found among the three activities.

Darch, Carnine, and Kameenui (1986) examined the effectiveness of a variety of instructional techniques with sixth graders in either individual or group structures. They reported a graphic organizer or SQ3R as more effective than a Directed Reading Approach, and group treatment more effective than individual treatment with both the organizer and SQ3R.

Jennings et al. (1983) reported on the teaching of a social studies unit for two weeks, during which time the experimental group of twelfth graders used structural organizers. Midway through the unit, they participated in a brainstorming activity that resulted in the construction of an overview of related terms and concepts. The control group received the assigned reading, lecture, and discussion. Learning and retention were tested using a criterion-specific unit test. No specific differences were found.

Karahaolios, Tonjes, and Towner (1979) used advance organizers and noted the effect on the comprehension by seventh graders of a chapter in a science text. Three treatment groups differed in the amount and kind of prereading instruction given. One was instructed to read the chapter and answer the questions at the end; the second was given the same initial direction and then instructed to skim the chapter first and attend to major headings and boldface or italicized vocabulary; the third received the same instructions as the others plus an advance organizer explaining major concepts. At the end of the week, students were given a comprehension test covering the material. A significant difference was noted between the first and third groups.

A number of researchers considered the value of using a structured overview in comparison with other methods prior to reading. Seidman (1984) compared the effectiveness of previewing and a structured overview as means of improving the reading comprehension of sixth graders. Following 17 instructional sessions over a five week period, both experimental groups scored significantly better than controls on passages accompanied by comprehension questions.

Carr, Dewitz, and Patberg (1983) found no significant differences when using the cloze procedure, a self-monitoring checklist, or a structured overview in teaching expository social studies materials to sixth graders. Dewitz, Carr, and Patberg (1987) investigated the effects of eight weeks of instruction using structured overview, cloze, and a combination of cloze and overview with fifth graders in social studies classes. Analysis of performance on comprehension measures revealed that the cloze procedure produced significantly better results for both literal and inferential comprehension; these same pupils evidenced higher metacognitive scores. Researchers emphasized that four weeks of instruction were necessary before results became evident.

In a comparison among four types of advance organizers (a paragraph abstract, an enumerated sentence outline, a true-false pretest, and a completion pretest), no significant differences were found with high school seniors (Proger et al., 1970) or sixth graders (Proger et al., 1973). When compared with SQ3R, the structured overview yielded higher scores among college undergraduates on a test of literal comprehension (Tonjes, 1981).

Cohen and Bradley (1977) investigated the efficacy of teaching superordinate concepts with simulation games and the subsequent effect on improvement in map reading skills. In the control group, fifth and sixth graders were taught facts and concepts directly within the context of a lesson on exploration. In the treatment group, subjects actively participated in the lesson by applying information from the lesson to a simulation task requiring them to use the new information to solve related problems. While there was no significant difference between groups on the map portion of the Iowa Test of Basic Skills when administered immediately following training, the treatment group did significantly better after two weeks.

Graves, Cook, and LaBerge (1983) studied the effects of giving detailed previews of short stories to seventh and eighth graders. Subjects received a preview of questions and statements concerning the story, a synopsis of the story in which characters were repeated, and three or four vocabulary words. Subjects who received the preview did significantly better on a multiple-choice test following the story. In an outgrowth of this study, all subjects then were asked to participate in the study with and without the preview using two new stories. Subjects recalled more than twice as many propositions when they received the preview as when they did not.

Several researchers investigated the differences in high school students' comprehension performance when using either verbal or graphic organizers. In two studies, graphic organizers presented key vocabulary in diagram form and discussed the terms. In both studies, comprehension was measured by a test on the material, and in both cases no significant differences were found (Barron, 1972; Barron & Cooper, 1973). Of concern also was the question of whether a pre or postgraphic organizer would be the best approach. Barron and Stone (1974) reported student-created postorganizers more effective than preorganizers.

Alvermann (1982) described a procedure for student reorganization of text and examined whether reorganized text aided by a graphic organizer would produce more recall of main ideas than the use of the text's top level structure. Tenth graders exhibited significant gains after training with the procedure. Alvermann and Boothby (1983) studied the effectiveness of a graphic organizer on the ability to retain textual material lacking in unity. Fourth graders in the experimental group recalled fewer of the irrelevant idea units than the control group, which received no special instruction.

These same investigators tested the effectiveness of graphic organizers on recall of main ideas. In addition to the regular classroom instruction, students in the experimental group received instruction with investigator-prepared graphic organizers designed to reflect either a comparison/contrast or a cause/effect structure. Written free recalls were used to assess comprehension and recall. Subjects in the experimental group immediately recalled significantly more idea units than did control group members. No differences were found between groups after a one month delayed recall (Boothby & Alvermann, 1984).

Bernard, Peterson, and Ally (1981) investigated the influence of two forms of prepassage organizers (contextual image or contextual written description) on reading performance. College students read passages from *Scientific American.* No notable difference was found between either of the organizers, but both were superior to no organizer. Sheldon (1984) found restructuring by means of diagraming an effective means of improving comprehension among 8 and 9 year olds. A worksheet was developed to provide practice in diagraming. Performance using the diagram worksheet was compared to the question-based worksheet provided for the control group. Subjects who had nonverbal restructuring made significant gains over those who used the question-answer methodology.

Sinatra, Stahl-Gemake, and Berg (1984) concentrated on the question of whether disabled readers, ranging from grades 2 through 8, given semantic map highlighting that included the structure and major events of a selection before reading, would understand and recall relationships better than when using a DRA. Subjects were assigned to read 10 selections; with 5 a DRA approach was used, and with the other 5 a map format was followed. The map format for each selection contained its key vocabulary and major concepts. The majority of students had higher comprehension scores when mapping. No significant differences were found when comparison was made among main idea, inferential, and detail questions.

Adjunct Questions

Golden (1942) compared 119 fifth and sixth graders reading questions prior to reading the passages on Durrell and Sullivan's New Standard Reading Test with 119 students reading the passages first and then answering the questions. Those who read the passage first made fewer errors, but the difference was not significant.

Using adjunct questions (AQs) with college texts, Frase (1968a, 1968b, 1968c, 1969) investigated the effects on learning of question location, question mode, length of passage, student motivation, and passage organization. Criterion tests about the content passages were used to determine whether the students learned (retained) the text information. His results consistently supported Rothkopf's notion that students' responses to direct questioning assist them in acquiring and retaining information. The specific results showed that learning and retention were facilitated by questions placed after the prose; by questions about relevant, not incidental, information; by questions placed after the text (they did not need to be as frequent as those before or within the text); by specific guide questions as compared with general guide questions; and by information organized by identifying concept attributes, not concept names. Frase (1971) found that factual information was recalled better than inferential.

Concerning the frequency of adjunct questions, Koran and Koran (1975) reported an experiment testing the relationship between verbal ability and retention of information with frequent, infrequent, and no inserted AQs. From each 20 pages of science text, two AQs were made to serve as measures of relevant learning. The questions were on separate sheets after each page (frequent) or after every four pages (infrequent). Undergraduates were told to read carefully and not to refer back to already read portions. A 40 item posttest was used to measure learning. The results showed that the groups with AQs did significantly better on the retention of relevant information; there were no significant differences between frequencies in questioning.

Boyd (1973) studied the effect of placement of one or five questions before or after one or five paragraphs. Ten experimental conditions and controls were set up with AQs about both intentional and incidental items. Two descriptive passages of 2,000 words were used on 20 separate pages with 4 AQs per page. In the pre and posttests, 40 of the questions were intentional (tested direct information in the paragraphs); 40 AQs tested incidental information and were used only in the posttest. The results showed that undergraduates responded significantly better on posttest intentional questions. The researchers felt the results supported their notion that repeated questions have an additive effect in that preconditions lead to selective attention to information.

Similarly, Swenson and Kulhavy (1974) examined the effect of questions in pre and postpositions on the immediate and delayed retention of fifth and sixth graders. Results indicated that AQs after the paragraphs were superior in facilitating retention as compared with those before the paragraphs and that relevant information was learned significantly better than incidental information. Working with tenth graders, Duchastel and Nungester (1984) compared the effects of questions placed at the end of a reading with the effects of questions interspersed through the reading when review of the materials was permitted after a question was encountered. There were no significant differences between treatments, but both were superior to the control group, which received no questions.

Felker and Dapra (1975) tested the effect of verbatim versus comprehension questions and pre and posttest position on a test requiring application of principles and concepts from the text. The comprehension postquestion group scored significantly higher; question placement did not produce significantly different results. Working with a similar sample of undergraduate psychology students, Wilhite (1983) found that recall of information was higher for passage segments containing information relevant to high level prequestions on passages hierarchically organized.

Prequestions and their effectiveness in aiding comprehension of cause-effect passages in social studies and science text materials were considered by Memory (1981, 1983). In both studies, low average and good readers in the sixth grade practiced responding to a variety of prestatements and prequestions. Test results from both studies indicated that good readers in the "no adjunct aid" group achieved a significantly higher mean score for main idea than did good readers in the application and "why" prequestion groups. For low average readers, however, "why" prequestions seemed to enhance understanding of main ideas.

Carnine et al. (1982) found that pupils in grades 4 through 6 gave more complete and correct responses following facilitative questioning in a postreading condition than if no intervention were offered. In a study involving college students in an introductory biology course, Doolittle (1981) distributed study questions one week prior to laboratory demonstrations. She found no significant difference between this group and those who had used another one of a number of study strategies previously presented in the course.

Gilmore (1978) examined the relationship between students' ability to comprehend general meanings and the teacher's use of a three part discourse structure in the discussion phase of a reading lesson. Teachers followed a competency-based teaching model consisting of a type of reciprocal questioning technique in which the teacher asked a question, the student responded, and the teacher reinforced the correct response by praising and repeating the answer. Teachers who made greater use of the structure enabled more students to infer the major themes of stories than did those using fewer instances of the three part discourse structure.

McCormick and Hill (1984) observed the effects of two procedures for increasing fifth graders' ability to draw inferences while reading. Individuals were assigned to one of three groups: (1) the strategy thrust, which offered opportunities to use previous experience in predicting story outcomes, (2) the question approach, which afforded practice responding to inference type questions, and (3) the control group, which followed traditional reading instructional practices. By the end of the second 5 week period, strategy group inference scores on end of story tests were significantly higher than those of the controls. By the end of the third and fourth 5 week segments, both the strategy and question groups' inference scores were significantly higher than those of the controls.

McGraw and Grotelueschen (1972) investigated the facilitative effects of AQs at intervals in prose materials. They studied both forward and backward effects on the comprehension of college students. For each of 21 pages, three questions were constructed: two related to details of the same material, and one dealt with an unrelated topic. The questions then were inserted at the end of different numbers of pages. The results showed no significant differences for forward or backward effects.

Richards and DeVesta (1974) analyzed the effect on college students' retention of different levels of questions inserted after every two or four paragraphs. Four types of questions were used: rote fact for specific facts in subordinate sentences, rote idea for literal information in superordinate sentences, meaningful questions requiring students to organize or subsume facts from subordinate sentences under ideas in topic sentences, and irrelevant questions. Results indicated that total recall after two paragraphs was highest, while rote ideas were superior to other question types in total recall. All task relevant questions made better relevant learning of facts than the irrelevant group, but there were no differences among question types.

A number of studies were conducted to ascertain what type of question would be most helpful in facilitating comprehension and retention of information. Rickards, Anderson, and McCormick (1976) examined the effects of different types of embedded questions on the learning of college students. Number and word questions showed equivalent recall irrespective of position in text. Rickards (1976) developed verbatim AQs from sentences rated as high or low in importance to the overall meaning/structure of the passage. College students then were given a high or low structural importance question either before or after related text paragraphs. A control group read the passage without any AQs. The results showed that the high structural importance pre and postquestion groups were equal in recall of the questioned statements, and both outperformed the reading only group. Friedman and Rickards (1981) also found inference questions superior to paraphrase questions, which, in turn, were superior to verbatim questions.

Reutzel (1984a) studied the effectiveness of adjunct story frames on the reading comprehension of fifth graders. Adjunct story frames were inserted in the margins of the passages at points in the text adjacent to the information pertinent to the adjunct story frame to be completed. Experimental group members were shown the story frame and asked to predict solutions to each frame. Then they read the story and completed the frames at the end of each paragraph. Control group members were given a directed reading activity in which they predicted responses to questions related to the passages. All subjects were asked for written free recall for each passage. No significant differences were reported for either procedure.

Cunningham et al. (1982) contrasted the relative efficiency of verbal adjunct aids with visual adjunct aids for concrete and abstract prose learning in college undergraduates. Verbal adjunct aids were multiple-choice questions interspersed in the text, and visual adjunct aids were directions to sketch pictures. Five versions of a series of passages were prepared: adjunct aids before the text selection for both concrete and abstract passages, adjunct aids after the text selection for both passages, and a control version with no adjunct aids. For the abstract passages, verbal adjunct aids showed a tendency to be more effective than directions to sketch. For concrete passages, no significant findings resulted for any interactions.

Holliday (1983) studied whether tenth graders receiving strong prompts to the answer of comprehension questions (adjuncts to a flow diagram) would comprehend less than those in a no prompt condition, whether only a flow diagram would outperform a strongly prompted diagram reading, and whether all treatments would outperform a control group. Although there were significant differences among the four groups in favor of the no prompt condition, further analysis failed to confirm the predicted descending order among treatment means.

Morse (1976) investigated the effects of interspersed questions on the reading of college students. Embedded questions were varied in two ways. They were either reader or researcher generated, and they were positioned either before, after, or before and after reading material. A 10 item multiple-choice test revealed no significant differences between groups when the means were adjusted for general reading ability. Students receiving researcher-generated questions in a passage condition significantly outperformed students getting reader-generated questions in the same passage condition.

Use of Objectives, Prequestions, Purposes

Kurtz (1974) compared learning of a prose passage by sixth graders who received instruction and practice in reading for recognition, recall, or application with those who were given no instruction. Performance on the Lorge-Thorndike Test of Verbal Intelligence indicated that practice in using instructional objectives had no significant effect on performance on the subtest measuring this ability.

Kaplan and Rothkopf (1974) found that the use of objectives as directions for reading resulted in increased performance by high school students. Working with a similar group, Kaplan and Simmons (1974) found no differences in students' performance because of placement (before or after the passage) or type (information specific and information nonspecific) of objectives. They found that relevant learning was significantly facilitated by objectives with directing information in the prereading spot, while objectives without directing information were most effective in the postreading spot.

Gagne and Memory (1978) examined reading comprehension following seven different types of prereading instructions. Sixth graders were directed to read carefully, form images, read a factual prequestion, read an application prequestion, read a main idea prequestion, read supplemental background, and read a supplemental causal relationship example. The hypothesis that prereading direction would influence significantly the nature of postreading comprehension was upheld for the factual prequestion condition. General comprehension was greater for imagery, application, and causal example.

Gagne and Britton (1982) identified how objectives for reading influenced the organization of information that college students recalled from text. Students given objectives after reading but before a review period had more clustering by objectives in free recall than did those who never saw objectives. Researchers often found that subjects improved in the area of the passage focused on, or the particular direction learning was expected to take, but reading comprehension was usually not improved by the presence of instructional objectives related to a passage (Glover et al., 1980; Winne, 1983).

Henderson (1965) presented stories to fifth graders in three ways: the pupils declared a purpose for reading a basal story, the researcher gave a purpose, or no purpose was given or developed. A rating scale was used to measure purpose-setting achievement and purpose attainment. Results showed a significant difference between those who set good purposes and those who set what were judged as poor purposes, but no significant differences were found among the three treatments. Jones (1976) studied the effect on comprehension of establishing purposes for reading and found that neither specific nor general purpose-setting directions significantly influenced sixth graders' overall achievement or level of achievement on intentional items. However, Babbs (1984) reported that a reading plan sheet and prompting comprehension cards were successful in increasing fourth graders' literal recall of content material. Grant and Hall (1968) appraised the value of giving sixth graders a broad, thought-directing question before reading a magazine article. Mean scores were greater for the experimental group receiving questions that focused on how something was alike or different.

Instead of the general purposes set by some researchers, Carney and Losinger (1976) offered specific directions in how to read materials to facilitate learning. Specific teaching included technical vocabulary training, organizational pattern recognition, priority determination through cue words, and organizing and remembering strategies. Junior college students in the experimental group scored significantly higher on the application of reading/study behaviors to an unfamiliar selection. Gagne, Bing, and Bing (1977) varied prereading instructions for high school students to determine how goal might affect organization of recall. Results showed that a combination of topic goals and an expectation for a completion test produced topical organization in free recall, while the combination of attribute goals and an expectation of a sorting test produced attribute organization in free recall.

LaPorte and Nath (1976) reported that more difficult goals resulted in longer study time after reading and produced higher performance by college students on tests. Blachowicz (1979) investigated the effect of directions for inferencing and the ability to complete a comprehension task. Working with readers ranging from second graders through adults, she found that the focus placed upon comprehension task significantly affected the emphasis and subsequent performance of readers.

Owens, Bower, and Black (1979) reported on the influence of undergraduate students' preset notions about character's motivations upon their interpretation and recall of narrative material. According to the results, providing the reader with the problem and motive of the character produced significantly more recall of text propositions.

Wiesendanger and Wollenberg (1978) examined the effect of prequestions on the comprehension of third graders and found that the control group, which received no questions, achieved the higher scores. However, the group receiving inferential prequestions achieved significantly higher than the group getting factual prequestions. Fowler and Lamberg (1979) found that there were no significant differences in comprehension as a result of pre or postquestion format. They concluded that elementary school pupils, unlike college students, may not take advantage of prequestioning because they are attending too much to the word recognition process.

Use of a Variety of Miscellaneous Means for Activating Schema

The following section includes studies investigating the use of embedded aids, question generation, and a variety of other means for activating prior knowledge.

Wright (1929) contrasted a motivated assignment with a nonmotivated assignment in an American history class of fifth and sixth graders, another of fourth and fifth graders, and another of sixth and seventh graders (no *N* stated). A test of background knowledge was given to all subjects. Motivation took two forms: subjects prepared a list of questions covering the assignment, and the teacher gave the class an outline for guided study. On an investigator-designed knowledge test, the experimental group gained 9.9 percent above the control group on subject-designed questions. When the teacher's outline was used, the experimental group surpassed the control group by 27 percent.

In 1931, Holmes conducted six experiments with 170 college students. One group was given 20 guiding questions, following the order of an article, to be answered during the reading. Another group read as many times as they could during a time limit. A test of the same 20 questions plus 20 others was given immediately after the reading and again two weeks later. A significant finding was that delayed recall for the guiding questions group was "strikingly superior." Holmes concluded that guided reading "facilitates the organization of what is read by eliminating mental groping for the more important points of the article" (p. 371).

Fridian and Rosanna (1958) worked daily for 24 sessions with 18 college students. Selections were from the European history text used in class; two to three minutes per session were spent on motivation and discussion of needed skills. There was an average gain in comprehension on investigator-designed tests from 66 percent at the start to 77 percent at the conclusion of the study.

Stevens (1981) studied whether direct instruction of background knowledge concerning topic resulted in increased comprehension. Tenth graders produced significantly better results on a second passage after reading one from the same topical area. Johnson (1982) reported similar results among university level ESL readers who received prior information concerning an unfamiliar topic in earlier paragraphs of a reading passage. Similarly, Hayes and Tierney (1982) reported the impact of an attempt to increase readers' background knowledge on the understanding of unfamiliar text. Significant increases in comprehension among eleventh and twelfth graders resulted from the analogy to baseball used to teach information about the game of cricket.

The facilitating effects of cues to prior knowledge about famous individuals was studied by Schustack and Anderson (1979). Undergraduate college students studied 42 short (four sentence) biographies of fictional characters analogous to famous people and then were tested on what they had read. Stories were written so that 28 of them gave a strong resemblance to the life of the person, while 14 did not. In the first phase of the study, results showed that the best recognition happened when the analogous famous person was identified at both the study and test phases. In contrast, the findings of the second phase indicated that this was not accurate: A famous person's name was beneficial only when facts in the biography were true of the person.

Neville and Hoffman (1981) investigated whether personalizing story material would increase the cloze comprehension scores of seventh grade retarded readers. Experimentals received a personalized form containing 68 words of immediate relevance to the reader; controls read the unaltered form of the story. Comprehension was measured by a cloze passage constructed from each passage. The mean of the experimental group was significantly higher than the mean of the control.

Flood (1978) gave eighth graders an initial sentence and asked them to supply a second sentence and facts expected in the remainder of the passage. He found readers' performances increased on passages containing familiar content, regardless of a violation of their expectations.

Hansen (1981) studied the effectiveness of special instruction on how prior knowledge could be used to draw inferences or make predictions about basal stories. Second graders in the control group spent comparable time getting story introductions as suggested by the teacher's guide. Findings on a comprehension test favored the experimentals. A prereading discussion requiring fourth graders to think of something they had done that was similar to the events in the text and to raise one or more hypotheses about what would happen, followed by a postreading discussion centered around 10 inferential questions, proved beneficial to poor readers but showed no effect on good readers (Hansen & Pearson, 1983).

While neither Meeks (1979) nor Manzo (1979) found significant differences in groups working with text-embedded aids, Siedow and Fox (1984) found that when tenth graders were trained to use description and comparison top level structures they improved significantly on measures of recall and comprehension.

Prosser (1978) examined the effects of relevant active questions as opposed to active and provided questions on the comprehension of pupils in middle school. The active question group was instructed to generate questions about the reading materials themselves; the provided question group wrote answers to questions given by the researcher; and the relevant active group wrote its own questions and then checked a list of the researcher's answers to identify those that answered the questions. They underlined the questions not answered. In short term comprehension, active questions were found to give greater help than questions provided by the researcher on the first presentation; relevant active questions were found to give the greatest improvement between the first and second presentations. In long term comprehension, both types of active questions proved to be as effective as provided questions. Overall, provided questions were found to be the most helpful.

Legenza (1978) reported the results of inquiry training on the reading/learning skills of seventh graders. Training procedures included the use of a wondering question to motivate the students; a request question in which students were asked a question about an object and had to generate other questions; a question-asking game for which the students constructed questions from a silent reading task; list questions for which the students had to provide examples through oral reading; information questions aimed at general information; and application questions for which students had to use questioning procedures in class situations. Students in the experimental group achieved significantly higher scores on a variety of questioning measures. Lucking (1976) found effective a questioning technique based on Bloom's taxonomy that explicitly sought to lead tenth graders to higher level questions and generalizations. Similarly, training in the use of the ReQuest procedure enabled students to ask more high level questions, and, as a result, their reading comprehension also improved (Larking, 1984).

Helfeldt and Lalik (1976, 1979) studied the impact of reciprocal and teacher questioning on the development of interpretive reading. In both studies, these researchers compared performances of fifth graders who dealt with questions given by teachers as opposed to questions formulated by both teacher and pupils. With the latter group, the teacher modeled and the pupils imitated the teacher's form of questioning. In the reciprocal question group, a correct response to a teacher's question permitted the pupil to ask a question of the teacher or to choose another pupil to do so. On standardized testing of reading comprehension, the reciprocal group scored significantly higher than the unilateral teacher questioning group. Carnine, Kameenui, and Woolfson (1982) found that fifth graders responded more accurately on transfer tests when they received training involving a prompted questioning strategy concerned with the identification of the problem statement and critical information in a story.

Chodos, Gould, and Rush (1977) conducted a pilot study to determine if teaching pupils to generate questions before reading, to write summary statements after reading, or to do a combination of the two would have any effect on fourth graders' immediate and delayed recall of social studies material. Pupil-generated questions were found to be most effective on both immediate and delayed recall. A.E. Smith (1973) trained seventh graders to generate their own questions prior to reading. He developed four lessons in which he taught students elements of the nature, type, and classification of questioning. Lessons moved toward the presentation of a passage, followed by students creating questions after previewing its title and subheadings. Students receiving the training demonstrated a greater ability to generate prereading questions. When Owens (1980) gave undergraduates an opportunity to prepare questions for assigned partners, their own comprehension improved significantly over that of those who did not generate questions.

Doctorow, Wittrock, and Marks (1978) examined the effect of sixth graders' generating original elaborative sentences on reading comprehension of passages containing no headings, one word headings, or two word headings. The combination of inserted paragraph headings and instruction in generating sentences about the story paragraphs approximately doubled comprehension and recall.

Dee-Lucas and Di Vesta (1980) examined the effects on learning from text when contexts were generated by college students or provided in text. In both a test of free recall and a test for knowledge of passage structure, readers who were taught to generate topic sentences recalled more than those who read text with provided aids.

In a study of seventh graders, Johnson and Bliesmer (1983) reported the effect of training students to generate their own questions while reading narrative text. Subjects who had been trained in narrative schema scored significantly better than those who responded to teacher-generated questions on multiple-choice questions following selections.

Cohen (1983) taught question generating through programmed materials and then asked for the application of the skill to short stories. Third graders receiving this training were better able to answer main idea questions and generate good questions for stories than the control group, which did not receive the instruction. Dreher and Gambrell (1985) studied whether children's learning of expository passages could be improved by teaching them to formulate questions on the main idea of paragraphs. Sixth graders received one of three treatments: (1) question instruction, in which subjects learned to formulate good questions; (2) question writing, in which subjects wrote questions but received no training on the appropriate kinds of questions to generate; and (3) read, recite, and review procedures. No significant differences were found for main effect of study technique.

Wong and Jones (1982) used a five step self-questioning technique to foster comprehension skills among learning disabled eighth and ninth graders. Subjects were asked to underline parts of a test passage they felt were important enough to be placed on a comprehension test. Training increased their awareness of important units as well as their ability to formulate good questions on those units.

Davey and McBride (1986) reported the effect on comprehension of training sixth graders to generate questions as opposed to merely requiring that students generate questions. On a posttest requiring students to generate two think-type questions and answer eight questions (four literal and four inferential), the question generation and question training groups outperformed the no question groups on literal questions. On inferential questions, the question training group exceeded all others.

Some researchers considered a model of generative learning for teaching reading in elementary schools. Linden and Wittrock (1981) found that instruction to generate, whether imaginal or verbal, produced significantly more text-related generations. While factual retention was not significantly influenced, relation of generations to story comprehension was significant. Along similar lines, Carnine and Kinder (1985) assessed the relative effectiveness of teaching schema-based question answering and generating images and summary statements with both narrative and expository prose. In the generative learning treatment, pupils in fourth, fifth, and sixth grades were asked to form an image, describe the image, and eventually summarize the entire passage. For the schema-based treatment, questions highlighted a story's structure by focusing on essential elements. Questions initially were asked by the teachers, and subjects later were reminded to generate questions as they read silently. Following training in both procedures, pupils scored significantly higher on comprehension questions and retellings.

Brooks et al. (1983) investigated the effectiveness of having college students generate their own headings for scientific text. Those who had been taught to generate headings had significantly higher scores on an essay content measure, an essay organization measure, and an outline content measure of performance.

Singer and Donlan (1982) taught 15 randomly assigned eleventh grade students to derive story-specific questions from schema-general questions as they read complex short stories. The control group read to answer questions posed beforehand by the teacher. Criterion-referenced tests administered after each of the six short stories resulted in statistically significant differences between the two groups.

Ritchie (1985) assessed the effects on reading comprehension of three types of instruction in main idea and question generation. Students in the first group were provided with modeling of the thinking involved in finding the main idea, prior to training in a self-questioning study procedure. Those in group two received training in a self-questioning study procedure without instruction in identifying the main idea. Those in the third group were given instruction in the language arts with little or no emphasis on reading comprehension. At the conclusion of the training, no significant differences were found on an uncued main idea test. On a cued main idea test, those in the first group outperformed the others. Significant relationships were found between the type of question generated and the training received, with those in the training in main idea group generating better questions than the others. A significant relationship was found between the quality of questions generated and scores on the uncued main idea test.

Balajthy (1986), working with college freshmen, offered training in the construction of self-generated questions, including recognition of paragraph topics, paragraph organization, and differentiation of the types of questions appropriate to various paragraph contents and structures. From mixed results among groups given varying amounts of training using a variety of materials, Balajthy concluded that self-generated techniques may be most effective only under specific questions.

Thematic preorganizers, a type of advance organizer intended to relate the main theme of the passage to the reader's background, were explored as adjunct aids for ninth graders in the understanding of expository text (Alvarez, 1983). Two supplemental aids were developed to accompany a two page selection from a ninth grade social studies text: a thematic preorganizer and a guided instruction exercise consisting of inferential statements read prior to a text and with which the reader must agree or disagree. There were no significant differences in the number of literal responses among treatment groups. Subjects receiving both treatments made significantly more inferred responses than subjects in either of the other groups. In two other studies, thematic organizers were found to enhance both literal and inferential comprehension among a variety of grade levels (Risko & Alvarez, 1983a, 1983b).

Reutzel (1984b) compared the efficacy of a story map versus discussion of oral/written questions as postreading treatments following basal reader stories for fifth graders. On a cloze passage, both treatments increased comprehension compared with the control group. In a similar study for teaching basal lessons, Reutzel (1985) presented steps for developing and evaluating story maps and then compared their effectiveness with that of the DRA. The mean number of propositions recalled by the story map group was significantly higher than the mean number recalled by the DRA group.

Tillema (1983) assessed the effectiveness of webteaching, a procedure for sequencing material that takes into consideration prior knowledge and the structure of the subject matter. Text conditions were crossed with the presence or absence of an external scheme (a graphic representation of the text's concepts). No significant effects for text type presentation were found among sixth graders, nor was there any interaction between text and prior knowledge. There were significant differences favoring the web text, but no differences with the external scheme.

Another technique for fostering students' directed reading was creating mental images. Most often, students were instructed to picture in their minds how something looked. Anderson and Kulhavy (1972) studied giving directions to high school seniors to form a vivid mental picture. Responses on a short answer test showed no significant differences in comprehension between groups as a result of instruction to create a mental picture, but the number of questions students answered correctly was directly related to questionnaire responses concerning the amount of imagery they reported. In a study involving fifth and sixth graders, Kulhavy and Swenson (1975) reported that pupils in an experimental group receiving mental imagery training recalled more semantic than verbatim test items.

Gambrell (1982) studied the effectiveness of induced mental imagery as a strategy for accessing prior knowledge in order to ease text-relevant predictions. First and third graders were directed to read stories that had been divided into five sections based on logical points in the story where predictions could be made about forthcoming events. At the end of each section, pupils were asked what they thought would happen next. Those in the experimental group were told to create pictures in their heads to help them remember what they read, while subjects in the control group were to think about what they read to help them remember. No differences were seen among the first graders. The third grade induced mental imagery group referred to significantly more facts and made more predictions than a control group.

Brody and Legenza (1980) explored whether college undergraduates' learning was affected by placement of illustrations and types of pictures. Subjects responded better to pictures placed after the reading and to pictures that represented an overview rather than a view of a single incident. In a similar study with undergraduates, Dean and Enemoh (1983) reported contrasting results. Pictures placed before the text allowed for much higher recall when subjects were asked to write everything they could remember about the passage.

Donald (1983) also examined the effectiveness of illustration in text. Working with readers in first, third, and fifth grades, he reported significant improvement in semantic acceptability of errors in oral reading accuracy but no significant effects for inferential comprehension.

Holliday (1981) offered high school biology students picture-word diagrams to improve comprehension. Performance on study questions led the researcher to conclude that encouraging students to focus on selected portions of critical information might interfere with more thorough understanding of the processes explained in the diagrams.

Text Structure

A number of researchers focused on whether instruction in the organizational patterns of text would favorably influence comprehension. Barnett (1984) investigated this possibility with college undergraduates enrolled in an introductory psychology course. Subjects received either a brief description of the organization of the text immediately prior to reading it or after reading but before recalling it, or they received no instruction. Half of each group read text that followed a research report form; the other half read text organized into a journalistic structure. The research report structure led to better performance than the journalistic structure. For both text structures, subjects getting instruction prior to reading did better on recognition and delayed free recall than subjects who received no instruction. Slater, Graves, and Piche (1985) also reported better performance when subjects received prior information about the organization of expository passages. A structural organizer plus outline grid produced better performance among ninth graders than an organizer without grid or than notetaking. Working with a similar sample of ninth graders, Slater (1985) found similar results for the organizer with grid for a variety of text structures.

Collins-Cheek (1983) taught seventh graders to identify and use four patterns of textual organization in their content area texts for one 30 minute period each day for 10 days. Subjects were taught an enumeration pattern consisting of circling the central thought and underlining information that expanded the idea. A relationship pattern was taught by underlining related ideas. A problem solving pattern involved subjects following and completing an outline. Subjects marked sentences that gave opinions to identify a persuasive pattern. No significant differences were found on any of the subtests of the Iowa Silent Reading Test when compared with those given to a control group.

Roller and Schreiner (1985) examined the effects of using narrative and expository organizational instruction on sixth graders' comprehension of prose. Subjects were assigned to four groups determined by crossing two levels of instruction—organizational and traditional—with two levels of text type—expository and narrative. Within instructional groups, subjects were assigned to either intact or scrambled testing conditions. Four forms of two passages were written: expository intact, expository scrambled, narrative intact, and narrative scrambled. Students who had the organizational instruction emphasis wrote better summaries than did those who had traditional instruction. The advantage, however, was present only when they worked with well-organized texts.

Research on the development of a schema for text structure often produced mixed results. Gordon and Braun (1982) indicated that fifth graders receiving training in story structure recalled significantly more propositions in text structure categories, answered correctly more questions concerning stories, and produced more text structure categories in the writing task. However, Dreher and Singer (1980) reported no significant differences among fifth graders in recall resulting from instruction in identifying the structure of a story. Using a similar sample, Sebesta, Calder, and Cleland (1982) found no significant results on recall following training in story grammar.

Spiegel and Fitzgerald (1986) offered direct instruction in story structure over a five week period to fourth grade less able readers, while a control group received instruction in word study and dictionary usage. At the conclusion of instruction, subjects completed a story production task and a scrambled story task, and they read two stories followed by literal and inferential questions. The story structure group outscored the control on comprehension tasks, were more willing to guess at information, and produced more complex and more fully formed stories.

Varnhagen and Goldman (1986) explored the effects on comprehension of teaching logical text relations to learning handicapped children. Over an eight week period, children were taught to identify story information categories and the causal relationships among them, to complete macrocloze exercises, to create story trees, and to create and respond to inferential questions about the causal relations in different stories. Comprehension was assessed using a variety of means, and on all of them, children improved on answering "why" questions, on memory recall questions, and on story structure questions.

Instruction in following expository text structure and verbalizing a macrostructure for expository text formed the basis for

Taylor's study (1982) of fifth graders. The experimental group received instruction in how to prepare and study hierarchical summaries for segments of their health text. Pupils in the control group received the usual classroom instructional procedures involving questions and answers from the text. During the eighth week of the study, subjects studied a passage from the same text and followed the procedure to which they had become accustomed. A test of recall indicated significantly higher scores for the experimental group. In a similar study, Brooks and Dansereau (1983) found evidence supporting the hypothesis that schema training significantly facilitated the processing of expository prose by an undescribed group of students.

Raphael and Wonnacott (1985) presented the results of experiments wherein fourth graders were taught to recognize the relation between the kind of comprehension questions and the answer sources (text or personal background) to be used. Following treatment, significant differences were found on correct and incorrect responses but not on match between response and location of information.

Reed (1968) investigated the relative effect of the study of syntax and paragraph structure on reading comprehension with monolingual and bilingual high school students. The experimental group received semiweekly instruction on 30 study sheets emphasizing comprehension through the study of syntax and paragraph structure. Specific indications of the content or method of presentation were not included. The control group used regular texts and library books. Achievement on the Nelson Reading Test favored the experimental group, with no significant differences between monolingual and bilingual students.

White, Pascarella, and Pflaum (1981) found significant results when using a sentence anagram/word grouping approach to improving sentence comprehension with multilevel learning disabled students. Greenewald and Pederson (1983) used a similar technique with second and third graders. The experimental group made significant gains on a cloze test measure of reading comprehension.

Hafner and Palmer (1980) studied the differential effects of teaching ninth graders to identify sentence kernels, logically analyze cognitive relationships, or understand vocabulary. Reading comprehension was significantly improved through sentence kernels and cognitive relationship training. Straw and Schreiner (1982) assessed how different methods of instruction in sentence structure in the area of writing affect student performance in language comprehension. Fourth graders received the usual textbook writing instruction followed by either sentence combining or sentence reduction. There was a significant treatment effect of the writing instruction on listening comprehension, reading comprehension as measured on a cloze test, and a syntactic maturity test. Sentence combining instruction yielded higher performance than sentence reduction or the textbook treatment.

Soltis and Pflaum (1979) studied the influence on seventh graders of instruction in the identification, meaning, and selection of syntactical connectives. Posttest comparisons showed significant superiority for the treatment group on the use of connectives but not on the McCall-Crabbs Standard Test Lessons. Similarly, Mavrogenes and Padak (1982) found that ninth graders improved significantly on syntactic measures after receiving training in language development consisting of exercises in syntactic manipulation. However, they showed no improvement on either the Gates-MacGinitie Reading Test or the Basic Reading Inventory.

Colwell (1982) presented to seventh graders a model for treating the paragraph as a semantic unit and processing the ideational relationships within it. The model consisted of three parts: direct teaching, functional application, and increased interaction with the text. The new procedure was compared with a DRA using social studies text material. Experimental subjects scored significantly higher on both reading and syntactical measures. Brozo, Schmelzer, and Spires (1983) studied whether researcher-improved chunking advantageously affected the comprehension of college undergraduates. In study 1, subjects were given an expository prose passage followed by 10 comprehension questions. For the chunked group, the article was divided into meaningful units by slash lines. In study 2, the subjects were given either the chunked or unchunked versions of a standardized test. In study 1, no significant differences were found; in study 2, a significant difference was found for good readers under the chunked condition.

Taylor and Beach (1984) studied the effects of instruction focusing on text structure in reading on the comprehension and recall of content area material with seventh grade social studies classes. In the experimental group, subjects received instruction and practice in how to produce and study a hierarchical summary of social studies material. After studying the summary, each subject related to another all that could be recalled from what had been read or written. In week seven of the study, subjects were asked to write recalls. The experimental procedure improved recall for unfamiliar but not for familiar material.

Kinney (1985) reported the development of a five day lesson sequence to teach first graders the expository structure of comparison/contrast using the language experience approach. The first day involved discussion of how objects were alike and different; the second day involved subjects in dictating a story to the teacher. The third and fourth days were devoted to practice activities related to the story, and the fifth day involved rearranging a scrambled version of a dictated story. Apparently, as a result of the training, more subjects made use of text structure to recall contrastive statements.

The cloze procedure, using the systematic deletion of words from text and replacement with a uniform blank line, was studied by a number of researchers. Schneyer (1965) examined the effect on the reading comprehension of elementary school pupils who received a series of 200-word cloze exercises from basal readers. Passages consisted either of deletion of every tenth word or deletion of alternate nouns and verbs. The exercises were completed, scored by the teacher, and returned to the pupils, who reviewed and corrected their answers individually. As measured on the Gates Reading Survey, no significant differences were found between the groups receiving the cloze activities and those receiving none. Guice (1969) compared the gains in comprehension, as determined by the Cooperative English Test, Reading Comprehension, of college students who received 16 cloze passages over the semester in a science course. There were no significant differences between the group receiving cloze activities and those receiving regular instruction only.

Kennedy and Weener (1973) studied the effect of individual training with the cloze procedure on third graders' reading and listening comprehension. The pupils were trained individually with printed or aural cloze procedure tasks. For the aural cloze training, a bell signaled a deleted word. One of two comparison groups received an individualized oral reading program, and the other remained in the regular class receiving no cloze instruction. The results of testing showed the visual training produced significant effects in listening and reading comprehension. The auditory training group showed significant effects on both reading and listening cloze tests.

Williams (1986) investigated whether instruction in dealing with text features might facilitate understanding for eighth graders in compensatory education classes. Students were taught to deal with the "ly" construction. Testing then was done to determine whether readers would do better with original texts or with text that had been modified for readability. Williams concluded that if readability is measured by formula, the adapted version is more readable; however, if readability is measured by reader comprehension, the original and adapted versions appear to be equal in readability.

Construction of structural organizers in the form of maps and flowcharts was used as a type of scaffolding to allow for ease in dealing with text structure. Geva (1983) trained community college students to represent prior knowledge and text structure in flowcharts. A significant improvement on the Nelson-Denny Reading Comprehension test was shown; a process analysis of experimental students' ongoing protocols pointed to qualitative changes in their flowcharts as well.

Carrell (1985), working with ESL students, indicated that training on the top level rhetorical organization of expository texts significantly increased the amount of information that 25 intermediate level students could recall.

Berkowitz (1986) compared two methods of instructing sixth grade students to use the organization of ideas in content reading as a framework for studying (map construction and map study procedures) with two control study methods that did not focus students' attention on text organization (question answering and rereading procedures). Results suggested that students in middle grade classrooms would benefit from instruction and practice in map construction.

Armbruster, Anderson, and Ostertag (1987) instructed fifth grade students in problem/solution text structure to ascertain whether it would improve their ability to learn from similarly structured material. Students were assigned either to a structure training group, which received direct instruction in recognizing and summarizing problem/solution text passages, or to a traditional training group, which merely read and discussed social studies passages. As measured by responses to a main idea essay question and by written summaries of two passages, students' ability to abstract the macrostructure of problem/solution text read independently was improved by the structure training. For the summarization tasks, the instruction was least effective for the low ability group, and the researchers concluded that instruction for this group should provide considerably more practice and feedback.

Braun and Gordon (1984) considered whether instruction in writing a narrative passage might aid in understanding the text structures used and thereby facilitate understanding of these passages. The teacher/investigator modeled the idea generation process on an overhead transparency. Significant improvement on the Gates-MacGinitie test led to the conclusion that writing instruction in narratives provides some input into the language data pool that manifests itself in the related process of reading.

Greenewald and Rossing (1986), working with fourth graders, compared the traditional basal reader paradigm of DRA with a modified DRA incorporating instruction in story grammar components and self-monitoring strategies. Despite the fact that the experimental group was asked to construct a map of the story, while the control group was tested using comprehension questions from the teacher's manual, Greenewald and Rossing concluded that a combination of story grammar instruction and self-monitoring training positively affects story comprehension.

Monitoring

Alessi, Anderson, and Goetz (1979) examined the influence of experimenter-induced lookback opportunities with college freshmen. The students read a text with inserted questions given on a computer, four lines at a time. The experimental group differed from the control group in that it received a lookback opportunity targeted to pertinent prior context when the inserted question was missed. Results did not support lookback facilitation of learning, but students receiving lookbacks showed better comprehension of later information dependent on prerequisite information. Garner and Hare (1984) found that, after instruction in using lookbacks to answer questions, the training was effective with subjects in the middle schools but not effective with high school subjects.

Raphael and McKinney (1983) studied the effects of training designed to heighten awareness of information explicitly stated in text, information implied by the text, and information found only in the individual's knowledge base. Training over six weeks consisted of teacher explanation, diagrams, and 50- to 100-word passages. The researchers found the training program helpful at both the fifth and eighth grade levels; prompting subjects to use their knowledge of question/answer relationships was helpful in the fifth grade, but disruptive among the older group.

Pflaum and Pascarella (1980) studied the effects of instruction designed to teach the use of context to determine the impact of errors on meaning. Subjects ages 8 to 13 were taught procedures for identifying errors and discriminating between those that affected meaning and those that did not. Another series of lessons was devoted to procedures for determining what self-corrections are, how they improve reading, what rules to use to correct errors, and how to use those rules. A third set of lessons concerned practice in oral reading and in the use of phonic cues. There were no main effects among the four treatments: errors and correction, errors and practice, correction and practice, and practice only.

Martin (1985) explored the effectiveness of self-questioning as a study technique for college freshmen. Subjects were questioned using a structured interview containing an assessment of how they processed information when they applied either the SQ3R technique or the REAP procedure and concerning what thought processes they used on one item they answered correctly and one item they failed to answer correctly.

Brown and Palincsar (1982) described the results of two intervention strategies, corrective feedback and strategy training, with 4 seventh graders identified as adequate decoders but poor comprehenders. Two of the subjects received corrective feedback prior to strategy training, with the order reversed for the other two. During strategy training, the experimenter and subject engaged in an interactive learning game that involved taking turns in leading a dialogue concerning each segment of text. The dialogue called for paraphrasing the main idea, discussing how information in a paragraph might be grouped, predicting possible questions that might be asked about a segment, hypothesizing about the content of remaining passage segments, and commenting on any confusions and how to resolve them. Corrective feedback followed by strategy training was the most successful sequence. Similar procedures and findings were reported by Palincsar and Brown (1984).

Davey and Porter (1982) reported a four-step instructional procedure aimed at elevating poor readers' comprehension by changing orientations to reading, focusing attention on meaning, self-generating criteria for understanding, and applying appropriate self-correcting strategies to improve comprehension. As a result of the procedure, middle school subjects were more successful in matching their perceived comprehension with their demonstrated comprehension. Grabe and Mann (1984) studied the effect of training on comprehension monitoring ability. Fourth and fifth graders played reading games in which they were asked to determine if prose statements were internally consistent or inconsistent. Significant differences were reported in comprehension monitoring skill. Short and Ryan (1984) reported the effectiveness of a story grammar strategy coupled with attribution training (designed to increase awareness of effort in efficient reading) for fourth graders classified as poor readers.

Reported awareness about reading and actual reading comprehension skills provided the focus of Paris and Jacobs' (1984) study of third and fifth graders. A structured interview task provided the data on the reading awareness of subjects. Four months of instruction were provided on how, when, and why to use reading strategies to enhance comprehension. Comparisons before and after instruction showed significant increases in subjects' awareness and use of comprehension strategies.

Garner et al. (1984) taught elementary level pupils who were "decoding proficient" to employ a text lookback procedure for the retrieval of unrecalled information. Subjects were taught why to use lookbacks as well as when and where to use them. There was evidence that text lookback instruction was needed, that it worked, and that effects were maintained over at least a five day interval.

Braun, Rennie, and Labercane (1986) employed conferencing with fifth graders in order to raise students' awareness of themselves as readers, to develop self-monitoring, and to improve overall comprehension. Students improved on the Gates-MacGinitie and in posttest conferences evidenced a heightened awareness of their own reading process.

Appendix B

References for Overview of the Research Reports

These references, in alphabetical order, represent all studies annotated in the Overview (Appendix A).

Abelson, A.G., and Petersen, M. Efficacy of "talking books" for a group of reading disabled boys. *Perceptual and Motor Skills*, 1983, *57*, 567-570.

Adams, A., Carnine, D., and Gersten, R. Instructional strategies for studying content area texts in the intermediate grades. *Reading Research Quarterly*, 1982, *18*, 27-54.

Alderman, G.H. The effect of certain kinds of drill exercises on comprehension. *Bulletin of the Extension Division*, Indiana University, 1923, *3*, 12-25.

Alderman, G.H. Improving comprehension ability in silent reading. *Bulletin of the Extension Division*, Indiana University, 1925, *11*, 28-37.

Alderman, G.H. Improving comprehension ability in silent reading. *Journal of Educational Research*, 1926, *13*, 11-21.

Alessi, S.M., Anderson, T.H., and Goetz, E.T. An investigation of lookbacks during studying. *Discourse Processes*, 1979, *2*, 197-212.

Alvarez, M.C. Using a thematic pre-organizer and guided instruction as aids to concept learning. *Reading Horizons*, 1983, *24*, 51-58.

Alvermann, D.E. Restructuring text facilitates written recall of main ideas. *Journal of Reading*, 1982, *25*, 754-758.

Alvermann, D.E., and Boothby, P.R. A preliminary investigation of the differences in children's retention of "inconsiderate" text. *Reading Psychology*, 1983, *4*, 237-246.

Anderson, R.C., and Kulhavy, R.W. Imagery and prose learning. *Journal of Educational Psychology*, 1972, *63*, 242-243.

Andrews, L. Directed reading question and cognitive organizer: Comparative effect on reading comprehension. *Research in the Teaching of English*, 1971, *5*, 79-83.

Andrews, L. Reading comprehension and three modes of prereading assistance. *Journal of Reading Behavior*, 1972-1973, *5*, 237-241.

Ankney, P., and McClurg, P. Testing Manzo's guided reading procedure. *The Reading Teacher*, 1981, *34*, 681-685.

Armbruster, B.B., Anderson, T.H., and Ostertag, J. Does text structure/summarization instruction facilitate learning from expository text? *Reading Research Quarterly*, 1987, *22*, 331-346.

Arnold, H.F. The comparative effectiveness of certain study techniques in the field of history. *Journal of Educational Psychology*, 1942, *33*, 449-457.

Aulls, M., and Gelbart, F. Effects of method of instruction and ability on the literal comprehension of short stories. *Research in the Teaching of English*, 1980, *14*, 51-59.

Austin, R. The study guide: An invaluable tool for content study and reading improvement. *Western College Reading Association Journal*, 1982, *2*, 3-4.

Babbs, P.J. Monitoring cards help improve comprehension. *The Reading Teacher*, 1984, *38*, 200-204.

Balajthy, E. The relationship of training in self-generated questioning with passage difficulty and immediate and delayed retention. In J.A. Niles and R.V. Lalik (Eds.), *Solving problems in literacy: Learners, teachers, and researchers*. Thirty-Fifth Yearbook of the National Reading Conference. Rochester, NY: National Reading Conference, 1986, 41-46.

Barnett, J.E. Facilitating retention through instruction about text structure. *Journal of Reading Behavior*, 1984, *16*, 1-13.

Barron, R.F. Effects of advance organizers and grade level upon the reception learning and retention of general science content. In

F.P. Greene (Ed.), *Investigations relating to mature reading*. Twenty-First Yearbook of the National Reading Conference. Milwaukee, WI: National Reading Conference, 1972, 8-15.

Barron, R., and Cooper, R. Effects of advance organizers and grade level upon information acquisition from an instructional-level general science passage. In P.L. Nacke (Ed.), *Diversity in mature reading: Theory and research*. Twenty-Second Yearbook of the National Reading Conference. Boone, NC: National Reading Conference, 1973, 78-82.

Barron, R.F., and Stone, V.F. The effect of student-constructed graphic organizers upon learning vocabulary relationships. In P.L. Nacke (Ed.), *Interaction: Research and practice for college-adult reading*. Twenty-Third Yearbook of the National Reading Conference. Clemson, SC: National Reading Conference, 1974, 172-175.

Barry, L., and Pratt, M. A remedial-reading program in a public high school. *School Review*, 1937, *45*, 17-27.

Baumann, J.F. The effectiveness of a direct instruction paradigm for teaching main idea comprehension. *Reading Research Quarterly*, 1984, *20*, 93-115.

Bean, T.W. The effect of a structured overview on university students' comprehension. *Western College Reading Association Journal*, 1981, *1*, 2-3.

Bean, T.W., and Steenwyk, F.L. The effect of three forms of summarization instruction on sixth graders' summary writing and comprehension. *Journal of Reading Behavior*, 1984, *16*, 297-306.

Beasley, C.E., Jr. A freshman reading program. *Journal of Developmental Reading*, 1959, *2*, 23-39.

Beauchamp, W.L. A preliminary experimental study of technique in the mastery of subject-matter in elementary physical science. *Studies in secondary education I*, Supplementary Educational Monograph No. 24. Chicago, IL: Department of Education, University of Chicago, 1923, 47-87.

Beck, I.L., Perfetti, C.A., and McKeown, M.G. Effects of long-term vocabulary instruction on lexical access and reading comprehension. *Journal of Educational Psychology*, 1982, *74*, 506-521.

Bennett, A.L. An experiment in reading. *Michigan Educational Journal*, 1953, *30*, 302-303. Also reported as Two experimental groups in reading. *College English*, 1954, *15*, 223-225.

Bennett, H.K. *A remedial program in reading involving the development of the basic study skills and their application to the content subjects* (unpublished report). Des Moines, IA: Department of Public Instruction, 1937.

Berger, A. Effectiveness of four methods of increasing reading rate, comprehension, and flexibility. *Perceptual and Motor Skills*, 1967, *24*, 948-950.

Berkowitz, S.J. Effects of instruction in text organization on sixth-grade students' memory for expository reading. *Reading Research Quarterly*, 1986, *18*, 161-178.

Bernard, R.M., Peterson, C.H., and Ally, M. Can images provide contextual support for prose? *Educational Communication and Technology Journal*, 1981, *29*, 101-108.

Bigler, J.K. Increasing inferential comprehension scores of intermediate-age mildly retarded students using two direct teaching procedures. *Education and Training of the Mentally Retarded*, 1984, *19*, 132-140.

Bird, G.E. An experiment in vocalization. *School and Society*, 1918, *8*, 569-570.

Blachowicz, C.L.Z. Factors affecting semantic constructivity in children's comprehension. *Reading Research Quarterly*, 1979, *14*, 165-181.

Blanchard, J.S. Preliminary investigation of transfer between single-word decoding ability and contextual reading comprehension by poor readers in grade six. *Perceptual and Motor Skills*, 1980, *51*, 1271-1281.

Boettcher, J.V. Computer-based education: Classroom application and benefits for the learning disabled student. In E.L. Hartwig (Ed.), *Annals of dyslexia*. Baltimore, MD: The Orton Dyslexia Society, 1983, 203-219.

Boodt, G.M. Critical listeners become critical readers in remedial reading class. *The Reading Teacher*, 1984, *37*, 390-394.

Book, W.F. How well college students can read. *School and Society*, 1927, *26*, 242-248.

Boothby, P.R., and Alvermann, D.E. A classroom training study: The effects of graphic organizer instruction on fourth graders' comprehension. *Reading World*, 1984, *23*, 325-339.

Bos, C.S. Getting past decoding: Assisted and repeated readings as remedial methods for learning disabled students. *Topics in Learning & Learning Disabilities*, 1982, *1*, 51-57.

Bottomly, F. An experiment with the controlled reader. *Journal of Educational Research*, 1961, *54*, 265-269.

Boyd, W. McK. Repeating questions in prose learning. *Journal of Educational Psychology*, 1973, *64*, 31-38.

Braam, L.S., and Berger, A. Effectiveness of four methods of increasing reading rate, comprehension, and flexibility. *Journal of Reading*, 1968, *11*, 346-352.

Braun, C., and Gordon, C.J. Writing instruction as a metatextual aid to story schema appreciation. In J.A. Niles and L.A. Harris (Eds.), *Changing perspectives on research in reading/language processing and instruction.* Thirty-Third Yearbook of the National Reading Conference. Rochester, NY: National Reading Conference, 1984, 61-65.

Braun, C., Rennie, B.J., and Labercane, G.D. A conference approach to the development of metacognitive strategies. In J.A. Niles and R.V. Lalik (Eds.), *Solving problems in literacy: Learners, teachers, and researchers*. Thirty-Fifth Yearbook of the National Reading Conference. Rochester, NY: National Reading Conference, 1986, 204-209.

Brody, P.J., and Legenza, A. Can pictorial attributes serve mathemagenic functions? *Educational Communication and Technology*, 1980, *28*, 25-29.

Brooks, L.W., and Dansereau, D.F. Effects of structural schema training and text organization on expository prose processing. *Journal of Educational Psychology*, 1983, *75*, 811-820.

Brooks, L.W., Dansereau, D.F., Holley, C.D., and Spurlin, J.E. Generation of descriptive text headings. *Contemporary Educational Psychology*, 1983, *8*, 103-108.

Brown, A.L., and Palincsar, A.S. Inducing strategic learning from texts by means of informed, self-control training. *Topics in Learning and Learning Disabilities*, 1982, 2, 1-17.

Brozo, W.G., Schmelzer, R.V., and Spires, H.A. The beneficial effect of chunking on good readers' comprehension of expository prose. *Journal of Reading*, 1983, *26*, 442-445.

Burks, J.D., and Stone, C.R. Relative effectiveness of two different plans of training in silent reading. *Elementary School Journal*, 1929, *29*, 432-436.

Callaway, B., McDaniel, H., and Mason, G.E. Five methods of teaching language arts: A comparison. *Elementary English*, 1972, *49*, 1240-1245.

Carney, J.J., and Losinger, W. Reading and content in technical-vocational education. *Journal of Reading*, 1976, *20*, 14-17.

Carney, J.J., Anderson, D., Blackburn, C., and Blessing, D. Preteaching vocabulary and the comprehension of social studies materials by elementary school children. *Social Education*, 1984, *48*, 71-75.

Carnine, D., and Kinder, D. Teaching low-performing students to apply generative and schema strategies to narrative and expository material. *Remedial and Special Education*, 1985, *6*, 20-30.

Carnine, D.W., Kameenui, E.J., and Woolfson, N. Training of textual dimensions related to text-based inferences. *Journal of Reading Behavior*, 1982, *14*, 335-340.

Carnine, D.W., Stevens, C., Clements, J., and Kameenui, E.J. Effects of facilitative questions and practice on intermediate students' understanding of character motives. *Journal of Reading Behavior*, 1982, *14*, 179-190.

Carr, E.M., Dewitz, P., and Patberg, J.P. The effect of inference training on children's comprehension of expository text. *Journal of Reading Behavior*, 1983, *15*, 1-18.

Carrell, P.L. Facilitating ESL reading by teaching text structure. *TESOL Quarterly*, 1985, *19*, 727-752.

Carroll, R.P. *An experimental study of comprehension in reading: With special reference to the reading of directions*. Contributions to Education No. 245. New York: Teachers College, Columbia University, 1926.

Center, S.S., and Persons, G.L. *Teaching high-school students to read: A study of retardation in reading*. New York: D. Appleton-Century, 1937.

Chodos, L.B., Gould, S.M., and Rush, R.R. Effect of student-generated pre-questions and post-statements on immediate and delayed recall of fourth grade social studies content. In P.D. Pearson (Ed.), *Reading: Theory, research, and practice*. Twenty-Sixth Yearbook of the National Reading Conference. Clemson, SC: National Reading Conference, 1977, 11-16.

Cline, M., Jr. A-V aids for Spanish-speaking pupils. In J.A. Figurel (Ed.), *Reading and inquiry.* Newark, DE: International Reading Association, 1965, 270-271.

Cohen, D.H. Effect of a special program in literature on vocabulary and reading achievement. In J.A. Figurel (Ed.), *Reading and realism*. Newark, DE: International Reading Association, 1969, 754-757.

Cohen, R. Self-generated questions as an aid to reading comprehension. *The Reading Teacher*, 1983, *36*, 770-775.

Cohen, R.B., and Bradley, R.H. Teaching superordinate concepts with simulation games. *The Alberta Journal of Educational Research*, 1977, *23*, 298-304.

Coles, P., and Foster, J. Typographic cueing as an aid to learning from typewritten text. *Journal of Applied Programmed Learning and Education Technology*, 1975, *12*, 102-108.

Collins-Cheek, M.D. An exploratory study of the use of organization patterns as an aid to comprehension. In G.H. McNinch (Ed.), *Reading research to reading practice*. Third Yearbook of the American Reading Forum. Athens, GA: American Reading Forum, 1983, 80-82.

Colwell, C.G. Paragraph processing: A direct-functional-interactive model. *Reading Improvement*, 1982, *19*, 13-24.

Coulter, M.L. Verbal problem solving in the intermediate grades. In J.A. Figurel (Ed.), *Reading and inquiry*. Newark, DE: International Reading Association, 1965, 303-306.

Courigan, M. Reading studies go to work. *English Journal*, 1942, *31*, 31-36.

Crawford, C.C. Relative values of reading and outlining as methods of study. *Educational Methods*, 1929, *8*, 434-438.

Crofoot, B.L. Remedial reading. *School and Society*, 1927, *25*, 205-206.

Cunningham, D.J., Snowman, J., Miller, R.B., and Perry, F.L.

Verbal and nonverbal adjunct aids to concrete and abstract prose learning. *Journal of Experimental Education*, 1982, *51*, 8-13.

Cunningham, J.W. Generating interactions between schemata and text. In J.A. Niles and L.A. Harris (Eds.), *New inquiries in reading research and instruction*. Thirty-First Yearbook of the National Reading Conference. Rochester, NY: National Reading Conference, 1982, 42-47.

Cunningham, P.M., Cunningham, J.W., and Rystrom, R.C. A new syllabication strategy and reading achievement. *Reading World*, 1981, *20*, 208-214.

Darch, C.B., Carnine, D.W., and Kameenui, E.J. The role of graphic organizers and social structure in content area instruction. *Journal of Reading Behavior*, 1986, *18*, 275-295.

Davey, B., and Porter, S.M. Comprehension-rating: A procedure to assist poor comprehenders. *Journal of Reading*, 1982, *26*, 197-202.

Davey, B., and McBride, S. Effects of question generation training on reading comprehension. *Journal of Educational Psychology*, 1986, *78*, 256-262.

Deal, R.W. The development of reading and study habits in college students. *Journal of Educational Psychology*, 1934, *25*, 258-273.

Dean, R.S., and Enemoh, P.A.C. Pictorial organization in prose learning. *Contemporary Educational Psychology*, 1983, *8*, 20-27.

Dearborn, W.F., and Wilking, S.V. Improving the reading of college freshmen. *School Review*, 1941, *49*, 668-678.

Dee-Lucas, K., and DiVesta, F.J. Learner-generated organizational aids: Effects on learning from text. *Journal of Educational Psychology*, 1980, *72*, 304-311.

Dewitz, P., Carr, E.M., and Patberg, J.P. Effects of inference training on comprehension and comprehension monitoring. *Reading Research Quarterly*, 1987, *22*, 99-121.

Doctorow, M., Witrock, M.C., and Marks, C. Generative processes in reading comprehension. *Journal of Educational Psychology*, 1978, *70*, 109-118.

Dolittle, K. Increasing student performance through questioning techniques. In G. Enright (Ed.), *Proceedings of the fourteenth annual conference of the Western College Reading Association.* Whittier, CA: Western College Reading Association, 1981, 38-43.

Donald, D.R. The use and value of illustrations as contextual information for readers at different progress and developmental levels. *British Journal of Educational Psychology*, 1983, *53*, 175-185.

Donald, M. The SQ3R method in grade seven. *Journal of Reading*, 1967, *11*, 33-35.

Draheim, M.E. Facilitating comprehension and written recall of exposition through DRTA instruction and conceptual mapping. In J.A. Niles and L.A. Harris (Eds.), *Changing perspectives on research in reading/language processing and instruction.* Thirty-Third Yearbook of the National Reading Conference. Rochester, NY: National Reading Conference, 1984, 167-172.

Dransfield, J.E. A technique for teaching silent reading. *Teachers College Record*, 1925, *26*, 740-752.

Dreher, M.J., and Gambrell, L.B. Teaching children to use a self-questioning strategy for studying expository prose. *Reading Improvement*, 1985, *22*, 2-7.

Dreher, M.J., and Singer, H. Story grammar instruction is unnecessary for intermediate grade students. *The Reading Teacher*, 1980, *34*, 261-268.

Duchastel, P.C., and Nungester, R.J. Adjunct question effects with review. *Contemporary Educational Psychology*, 1984, *9*, 97-103.

Dunman, L. Preview summaries and coding: Aids in the identification of main ideas with normal and retarded subjects. *Journal of Research and Development in Education*, 1973, *6*, 65-70.

Dutton, R. The mediation of three-dimensional visualization for isolinal graphics. *British Journal of Educational Technology*, 1978, *9*, 211-216.

Dyer, J.W., Riley, J., and Yekovich, F.P. An analysis of three study skills: Notetaking, summarizing, and rereading. *Journal of Educational Research*, 1979, *73*, 3-7.

Eanet, M.G. An investigation of the REAP reading/study procedure: Its rationale and efficacy. In P.D. Pearson and J. Hansen (Eds.), *Reading: Disciplined inquiry in process and practice*. Twenty-Seventh Yearbook of the National Reading Conference. Clemson, SC: National Reading Conference, 1978, 229-232.

Eisenhart, W.W. *Remedial measures in reading*. Seventh Annual Schoolmen's Week Proceedings. Philadelphia, PA: University of Pennsylvania, 1920, 212-215.

Englert, C.S., and Lichter, A. Using statement-pie to teach reading and writing skills. *Teaching Exceptional Children*, 1982, *14*, 164-170.

Eurich, A.C. *The reading abilities of college students: An experimental study*. Minneapolis, MN: University of Minnesota Press, 1931.

Farbish, S.A. An experiment in remedial reading. *English Journal*, 1933, *22*, 585-587.

Farrell, E. SSR as the core of a junior high reading program. *Journal of Reading*, 1982, *26*, 48-51.

Felker, D.B., and Dapra, R.A. Effects of question type and question placement on problem-solving ability from prose material. *Journal of Educational Psychology*, 1975, *67*, 380-384.

Fitzgerald, J., and Spiegel, D. Enhancing children's reading comprehension through instruction in narrative structure. *Journal of Reading Behavior,* 1983, *12,* 1-17.

Fleisher, L.S., and Jenkins, J.R. The effect of word-and comprehension-emphasis instruction on reading performance. *Learning Disability Quarterly*, 1983, *6*, 146-154.

Fleisher, L.S., Jenkins, J.R., and Pany, D. Effects on poor readers' comprehension of training in rapid decoding. *Reading Research Quarterly*, 1979, *15*, 30-48.

Flood, J.E. The influence of first sentences on reader expectations within prose passages. *Reading World*, 1978, *17*, 306-315.

Fowler, E.D., and Lamberg, W.J. Effect of pre-questions on oral reading by elementary students. *Reading Improvement*, 1979, *16*, 71-74.

Fowler, R.L., and Barker, A.S. Effectiveness of highlighting for retention of text material. *Journal of Applied Psychology*, 1974, *59*, 358-364.

Frase, L.T. Cybernetic control of memory while reading connected discourse. *Journal of Educational Psychology*, 1969, *60*, 49-55.

Frase, L.T. Effect of incentive variables and type of adjunct question upon text learning, *Journal of Educational Psychology*, 1971, *62*, 371-375.

Frase, L.T. Effect of question location, pacing, and mode upon retention of prose material. *Journal of Educational Psychology*, 1968a, *59*, 244-249.

Frase, L.T. Some data concerning the mathemagenic hypothesis. *American Educational Research Journal*, 1968b, *5*, 181-189.

Frase, L.T. Some unpredicted effects of different questions upon learning from connected discourse. *Journal of Educational Psychology*, 1968c, *59*, 197-201.

French, L.C. The effect on achievement in geography of specific training in vocabulary; the reading of maps, graphs, and tables; and organization. *University of Pittsburgh Bulletin*, 1933, *29*, 83-92.

Fridian, M., and Rosanna, M. A developmental reading experiment in European history class. *Journal of Developmental Reading*, 1958, *1*, 3-7.

Friedman, F., and Rickards, J.P. Effect of level, review, and sequence of inserted questions on text processing. *Journal of Educational Psychology*, 1981, *73*, 427-436.

Froese, V., and Kurushima, S. The effects of sentence expansion practice on the reading comprehension and writing ability of third-graders. In M.L. Kamil and A.J. Moe (Eds.), *Reading research: Studies and applications*. Twenty-Eighth Yearbook of the National Reading Conference. Clemson, SC: National Reading Conference, 1979, 95-99.

Gagne, E.D., and Britton, B.K. The role of objectives in guiding the organization of information learned from text. *Contemporary Educational Psychology*, 1982, *7*, 15-25.

Gagne, E.D., and Memory, D. Instructional events and comprehension: Generalization across passages. *Journal of Reading Behavior*, 1978, *10*, 321-335.

Gagne, E.D., Bing, S.B., and Bing, J.R. Combined effect of goal organization and test expectations on organization in free recall following learning from text. *Journal of Educational Psychology*, 1977, *69*, 428-431.

Gambrell, L.B. Induced mental imagery and the text prediction performance of first and third graders. In J.A. Niles and L.A. Harris (Eds.), *New inquiries in reading research and instruction*. Thirty-First Yearbook of the National Reading Conference. Rochester, NY: National Reading Conference, 1982, 131-135.

Garner, R., and Hare, V.C. Efficacy of text lookback training for poor comprehenders at two age levels. *Journal of Educational Research*, 1984, *77*, 376-381.

Garner, R., Hare, V.C., Alexander, P., Haynes, J., and Winograd, P. Inducing use of a text lookback strategy among unsuccessful readers. *American Educational Research Journal*, 1984, *21*, 789-798.

Gates, A.I. Study of depth and rate of comprehension in reading by means of a practice experiment. *Journal of Educational Research*, 1923, *7*, 37-49.

Gates, A.I., and Van Alstyne, D. The general and specific effects of training in reading with observations on the experimental technique. *Teachers College Record*, 1924, *25*, 98-123.

Gatto, F.M. The effect of parallel reading in history. *University of Pittsburgh School of Education Journal*, 1927, *2*, 3-8.

Gatto, F.M. Remedial reading in Pittsburgh high schools. *Pittsburgh Schools*, 1934, *9*, 3-12.

Gelzer, A., and Santore, N. A comparison of various reading improvement approaches. *Journal of Educational Research*, 1968, *61*, 267-272.

Germane, C.E. Outlining and summarizing compared with re-reading as methods of studying. In G.M. Whipple (Ed.), *Report of the society's committee on silent reading*. Twentieth Yearbook of the National Society for the Study of Education, Part 2. Bloomington, IL: Public School Publishing, 1921d, 103-113.

Germane, C.E. The value of the controlled mental summary as a method of studying. *School and Society*, 1920, *12*, 591-593.

Germane, C.E. The value of the controlled summary as a method of studying. *School and Society*, 1921a, *13*, 730-732.

Germane, C.E. The value of the corrected summary as compared with the re-reading of the same article. *Elementary School Journal*, 1921b, *21*, 461-464.

Germane, C.E. The value of the written paragraph summary. *Journal of Educational Research*, 1921c, *3*, 116-123.

Gersten, R., and Carnine, D. Direct instruction in reading comprehension. *Educational Leadership*, 1986, *43*, 70-78.

Geva, E. Facilitating reading comprehension through flowcharting. *Reading Research Quarterly*, 1983, *18*, 384-405.

Gilmore, S. The use of discourse analysis in teaching an inferential reading comprehension skill. *Journal of Research in Reading*, 1978, *1*, 128-135.

Glover, J.A., Zimmer, J.W., Filbeck, R.W., and Plake, B.S. Effects of training students to identify the semantic base of prose materials. *Journal of Applied Behavior Analysis*, 1980, *13*, 655-667.

Glover, J.A., Zimmer, N.W., Ronning, R.R., and Petersen, C.H. Nobody knows how to remember that prose. *Journal of Educational Research*, 1980, *73*, 340-343.

Goldberg, M.A. Can reading ability be improved more effectively through wide reading or intensive drill? *High Points*, 1946, 21-27.

Golden, M.L. Reading guided by questions versus careful reading followed by questions. *Journal of Educational Psychology*, 1942, *33*, 463-468.

Good, C.V. The effect of extensive and intensive reading on the reproduction of ideas or thought units. *Journal of Educational Psychology*, 1927, *18*, 477-485.

Good, C.V. The effect of single reading versus two readings of a given body of material. *Journal of Educational Method*, 1926, *5*, 325-329.

Gordon, C.J., and Braun, C. Story schemata: Metatextual aid to reading and writing. In J.A. Niles and L.A. Harris (Eds.), *New inquiries in reading research and instruction*. Thirty-First Yearbook of the National Reading Conference, 1982. Rochester, NY: National Reading Conference, 1982, 262-268.

Grabe, M. Utilization of imposed structure: The impact of reading competence and grade level. *Journal of Reading Behavior*, 1980, *12*, 31-40.

Grabe, M., and Mann, S. A technique for the assessment and training of comprehension monitoring skills. *Journal of Reading Behavior*, 1984, *16*, 131-144.

Grant, E.B., and Hall, M. The effect of a thought-directing question on reading comprehension at differing levels of difficulty. In J.A. Figurel (Ed.), *Forging ahead in reading*. Newark, DE: International Reading Association, 1968, 498-501.

Graves, M.F., Cooke, C.L., and Laberge, M.J. Effects of previewing difficult short stories on low ability junior high school students' comprehension, recall, and attitudes. *Reading Research Quarterly*, 1983, *18*, 262-276.

Gray, W.S. *The use of tests in diagnosis and remedial work, with special reference to reading and study habits*. Report of the thirteenth meeting of the American College Personnel Association. Lafayette, IN: American College Personnel Association, 1936, 22-27.

Greene, H.A. Directed drill in the comprehension of verbal problems in arithmetic. *Journal of Educational Research*, 1925, *11*, 33-40.

Greenewald, M.J., and Pederson, C. Effects of sentence organization instruction on the reading comprehension of poor readers. In J.A. Niles and L.A. Harris (Eds.), *Searches for meaning in reading/language processing and instruction*. Thirty-Second Yearbook of the National Reading Conference. Rochester, NY: National Reading Conference, 1983.

Greenewald, M.J., and Rossing, R.L. Short-term and long-term effects of story grammar and self-monitoring training on children's story comprehension. In J.A. Niles and R.V. Lalik (Eds.), *Solving problems in literacy: Learners, teachers, and researchers*. Thirty-Fifth Yearbook of the National Reading Conference. Rochester, NY: National Reading Conference, 1986, 210-213.

Grobel, L. A comparison of two strategies in the teaching of reading comprehension. *English Language Teaching Journal*, 1979, *33*, 306-309.

Guice, B.M. The use of the cloze procedure for improving reading comprehension of college students. *Journal of Reading Behavior*, 1969, *1*, 81-92.

Guiler, W.S., and Coleman, J.H. Reading at the college level. *Journal of the American Association of Collegiate Registrars*, 1941, *17*, 16-27.

Gumlick, H.R., and Allphin, H. Improving ability to interpret stories. *Denver Public Schools Bulletin*, 1931, *4*, 2-4.

Hafner, E., and Palmer, B.C. The differential effects of three methods of teaching on the reading comprehension and vocabulary of ninth grade students. *Journal of Educational Research*, 1980, *74*, 34-37.

Hansen, J. An inferential comprehension strategy for use with primary grade children. *The Reading Teacher*, 1981, *34*, 665-669.

Hansen, J., and Pearson, P.D. An instructional study: Improving the inferential comprehension of good and poor fourth-grade readers. *Journal of Educational Psychology*, 1983, *75*, 821-829.

Hare, V.C., and Borchardt, K.M. Direct instruction of summarization skills. *Reading Research Quarterly*, 1984, *20*, 62-78.

Hayes, D.A., and Readence, J.E. Effects of cued attention to illustrations in text. In J.A. Niles and L. Harris (Eds.), *New inquiries in reading research and instruction*. Thirty-First Yearbook of the National Reading Conference. Rochester, NY: National Reading Conference, 1982, 60-63.

Hayes, D.A., and Readence, J.E. Transfer of learning from illustration-dependent text. *Journal of Educational Research*, 1983, *76*, 245-248.

Hayes, D.A., and Tierney, R.J. Developing readers' knowledge through analogy. *Reading Research Quarterly*, 1982, *17*, 256-280.

Heckelman, R.G. A neurological-impress method of remedial-reading instruction. *Academic Therapy*, 1969, *4*, 277-282.

Helfeldt, J.P., and Lalik, R. Reciprocal student-teacher questioning. *The Reading Teacher*, 1976, *30*, 283-287.

Helfeldt, J.P., and Lalik, R. Reciprocal student-teacher questioning. In C. Pennock (Ed.), *Reading comprehension at four linguistic levels*. Newark, DE: International Reading Association, 1979, 74-79.

Helseth, I.O. *Children's thinking: A study of the thinking done by a group of grade school children when encouraged to ask ques-*

tions about United States history. Contributions to Education No. 209. New York: Bureau of Publications, Teachers College, Columbia University, 1926.

Henderson, E.H. A study of individually formulated purposes for reading. *Journal of Educational Research*, 1965, *58*, 438-441.

Hicks, G.M., Jr. Sustained silent reading as an aid to reading achievement: A personal study. *New England Reading Association Journal*, 1983, *18*, 24-28.

Hill, W.R. Influence of direction upon the reading flexibility of advanced college readers. In E.L. Thurstone and L.E. Hafner (Eds.), *New concepts in college-adult reading*. Thirteenth Yearbook of the National Reading Conference. Milwaukee, WI: National Reading Conference, 1964.

Hislop, G.R. A study of division two social studies reading skills. *Alberta Journal of Educational Research*, 1961, *7*, 28-38.

Holliday, W.G. Overprompting science students using adjunct study questions. *Journal of Research in Science Teaching*, 1983, *20*, 195-201.

Holliday, W.G. Selective attentional effects of textbook study questions on student learning in science. *Journal of Research in Science Teaching*, 1981, *18*, 282-289.

Holmes, E. Reading guided by questions versus careful reading and re-reading without questions. *School Review*, 1931, *34*.

Hoon, P.W. Efficacy of three common study methods. *Psychological Reports*, 1974, *35*, 1057-1058.

Hoover, J.H. Motivated drill work in third-grade silent reading. In G.M. Whipple (Ed.), *Report of the society's committee on silent reading*. Twentieth Yearbook of the National Society for the Study of Education, Part 2. Bloomington, IL: Public School Publishing, 1921, 77-89.

Idstein, P., and Jenkins, J.R. Underlining versus repetitive reading. *Journal of Educational Research*, 1972, *65*, 321-323.

Jacobson, P.B. Two experiments with work-type reading exercises in ninth grade. *University of Iowa Studies in Education*, 1933, *8*, 1-85.

Jacobson, P.B., and Van Dusen, E.C. Remedial instruction in reading in the ninth grade. *School Review*, 1930, *38*, 142-146.

Jacques, R.Y. Using college reading assignments to improve reading/thinking skills. *Reading Horizons*, 1982, *22*, 282-287.

Jacques, R.Y., and Corrin, J.P. Reading improvement: A collegiate approach. *New England Reading Association Journal*, 1981, *16*, 17-20.

James, M.E. Using the results of measurement in reading in training student-teachers. *Elementary School Journal*, 1922, *23*, 190-196.

Jennings, R., McNinch, G., Germes, S., and Germes, S. Research application of schema theory in a twelfth-grade classroom. In G.H. McNinch (Ed.), *Reading research to reading practice*. Third Yearbook of the American Reading Forum. Athens, GA: University of Georgia, 1983, 132-134.

Johnson, G.S., and Bliesmer, E.P. Effects of narrative schema training and practice in generating questions on reading comprehension of seventh grade students. In G.H. McNinch (Ed.), *Reading research to reading practice*. Third Yearbook of the American Reading Forum. Athens, GA: University of Georgia, 1983, 91-94.

Johnson, P. Effects on reading comprehension of building background knowledge. *TESOL Quarterly*, 1982, *16*, 503-516.

Johnston, J.S., Coleman, J.H., and Guiler, W.S. Improving the reading ability of elementary-school pupils. *Elementary School Journal*, 1941, *42*, 105-115.

Jones, M.B. The effect of specificity of reading purposes on children's reading achievement. *Journal of Reading Behavior*, 1976, *8*, 405-416.

Jones, R.L., and Van Why, E.L. The SRA reading laboratory and fourth grade pupils. *Journal of Developmental Reading*, 1961, *5*, 36-46.

Joseph, N. Integrated language skills: An approach to development studics. *Forum for Reading*, 1984, *16*, 32-35.

Kaplan, R., and Rothkopf, E.Z. Instructional objectives as directions to learners: Effect of passage length and amount of objective-relevant content. *Journal of Educational Psychology*, 1974, *66*, 448-456.

Kaplan, R., and Simmons, F.G. Effects of instructional objectives used in orienting stimuli or as summary/review upon prose learning. *Journal of Educational Psychology*, 1974, *66*, 614-622.

Karahalios, S.M., Tonjes, M.J., and Towner, J.C. Using advance organizers to improve comprehension of content text. *Journal of Reading*, 1979, *22*, 706-708.

Keener, F.F. How to study in high school. *Chicago Schools Journal*, 1929, *11*, 167-169.

Kefford, R. Assessing reading gains in a scheme based on sustained silent reading. *Australian Journal of Reading*, 1981, *4*, 212-216.

Kendrick, W.M. A comparative study of two first grade language arts programs. *The Reading Teacher*, 1966, *20*, 25-30.

Kennedy, D.K., and Weener, P. Visual and auditory training with the cloze procedure to improve reading and listening comprehension. *Reading Research Quarterly*, 1973, *8*, 524-541.

Kennon, C.H., and Noland, R.G. Utilizing moral dilemmas to enhance comprehension. *Reading Improvement*, 1983, *20*, 75-80.

King, J.R., Biggs, S., and Lipsky, S. Students' self-questioning and summarizing as reading study strategies. *Journal of Reading Behavior*, 1984, *16*, 205-218.

Kinney, M.A. A language experience approach to teaching expository text structure. *The Reading Teacher*, 1985, *38*, 854-856.

Koran, M.L., and Koran, J.J., Jr. Interaction of learner aptitudes with question pacing in learning from prose. *Journal of Educational Psychology*, 1975, *67*, 76-82.

Kulhavy, R.W., and Swenson, I. Imagery instructions and the comprehension of text. *British Journal of Educational Psychology*, 1975, *45*, 47-51.

Kurtz, P.D. The effect of instructional objectives on student learning. *The Alberta Journal of Educational Research*, 1974, *20*, 327-333.

Laffey, J.L., and Kelly, D. Repeated readings of taped literature: Does it make a difference? In G.H. McNinch (Ed.), *Comprehension: Process and product*. First Yearbook of the American Reading Forum. Athens, GA: University of Georgia, 1981, 80-83.

Laffey, J.L., Kelly, D., and Perry, B. The effect of repeated reading of taped literature on reading achievement. In M.L. Kamil and A.J. Moe (Eds.), *Perspectives on reading research and instruc-*

tion. Twenty-Ninth Yearbook of the National Reading Conference. Washington, DC: National Reading Conference, 1980, 189-193.

Lamoreaux, L.A., Farley, R., Herring, B., and Trott, F. Remedial reading instruction in sixth grade groups. *California Journal of Elementary Education*, 1934, *3*, 116-122.

LaPorte, R.E., and Nath, R. Role performance goals in prose learning. *Journal of Educational Psychology*, 1976, *68*, 260-264.

Larking, L. ReQuest helps children comprehend: A study. *Australian Journal of Reading*, 1984, *7*, 135-139.

Legenza, A. Inquiry training for reading and learning improvement. *Reading Improvement*, 1978, *15*, 309-316.

Lemons, R.L., and Malatesha, R.N. Improving reading through training to listen. *Perceptual and Motor Skills*, 1985, *60*, 788-790.

Lemons, R.L., and Moore, S.C. The effects of training in listening on the development of reading skills. *Reading Improvement*, 1982, *19*, 212-216.

Lessenger, W.E. Reading difficulties in arithmetical computation. *Journal of Educational Research*, 1925, *11*, 287-291.

Limb, G., and Parker, H.T. An experiment in the teaching of reading comprehension. *Australian educational studies*, Educational Research Series, No. 14. Melbourne, Australia: Melbourne University Press, 1932, 30-51.

Linden, M., and Wittrock, M.C. The teaching of reading comprehension according to the model of generative learning. *Reading Research Quarterly*, 1981, *17*, 44-57.

Livingston, H. An investigation of the effect of instruction in general semantics on critical reading ability. *California Journal of Educational Research*, 1965, *16, 93-96.*

Lorenz, L., and Vockell, E. Using the neurological impress method with learning disabled readers. *Journal of Learning Disabilities*, 1979, *12*, 420-422.

Lowerre, G.F., and Scandura, J.M. Conceptually based development and evaluation of individualized materials for critical reading based on logical inference. *Reading Research Quarterly*, 1974, *9*, 186-205.

Lucking, R.A. A study of the effects of a hierarchically-ordered questioning technique on adolescents' responses to short stories. *Research in the Teaching of English*, 1976, *10*, 269-276.

Lynch, C.F. Corrective practice with a slow group in silent reading. *Chicago Schools Journal*, 1924, *6*, 135-139.

Maddison, J.M., and Rimmington, G.T. The improvement of reading: An experimental study. *Canadian Education and Research Digest*, 1966, *6*, 188-190.

Manning, G.L., and Manning, M. What models of recreational reading make a difference? *Reading World*, 1983, *23*, 375-380.

Manzo, A.V. Embedded aids to readers: Alternative to traditional textual materials. *New England Reading Association Journal*, 1979, *14*, 13-18.

Marshall, N. The effects of differential instruction on story comprehension. *Florida Reading Quarterly*, 1984, *20*, 3-7.

Martens, M. The role of a pacer in improving comprehension. *Journal of Developmental Reading*, 1961, *4*, 135-139.

Martin, M.A. Students' application of self-questioning techniques: An investigation of their efficacy. *Reading Psychology*, 1985, *6*, 69-85.

Mathews, C.D. Comparison of methods of study for immediate and delayed recall. *Journal of Educational Psychology*, 1938, *29*, 101-106.

Mavrogenes, N.A., and Padak, N.D. The reading road to writing. *Journal of Educational Research*, 1982, *75*, 354-359.

Mayhew, J.B., and Weaver, C.H. Four methods of teaching reading improvement at the college level. *Journal of Developmental Reading*, 1960, *3*, 75-83.

McCallister, J.M. College instruction in reading. *Phi Delta Kappan*, 1942, *24*, 311-313.

McCallister, J.M., and Baker, G.H. Corrective instruction in reading in seventh-grade English classes. *English Journal*, 1932, *21*, 734-743.

McCarty, P.S. Increasing comprehension in silent reading. *School Review*, 1931, *39*, 758-766.

McCormick, S., and Hill, D.S. An analysis of the effects of two procedures for increasing disabled readers' inferencing skills. *Journal of Educational Research*, 1984, *77*, 219-226.

McCullough, C. Improving reading comprehension in grade IX. *School Review*, 1937, *45*, 266-273.

McDonald, A.S., and Pauk, W.J. Teaching college freshmen to read. *Phi Delta Kappan*, 1956, *38*, 104-109.

McDowell, N.A. The effectiveness of the controlled reader in developing reading rate, comprehension, and vocabulary as opposed to the regular method of teaching reading. *Journal of Experimental Education*, 1964, *32*, 363-369.

McGraw, B., and Grotelueschen, A. Direction of the effect of questions in prose material. *Journal of Educational Psychology*, 1972, *63*, 580-588.

McKeown, M.G., Beck, I.L., Omanson, R.C., and Perfetti, C.A. The effects of long-term vocabulary instruction on reading comprehension: A replication. *Journal of Reading Behavior*, 1983, *15*, 3-18.

McNeil, J., and Donant, L. Summarization strategy for improving reading comprehension. In J.A. Niles and L.A. Harris (Eds.), *New inquiries in reading research and instruction*. Thirty-First Yearbook of the National Reading Conference. Rochester, NY: National Reading Conference, 1982, 215-219.

Meade, R.A. An eighth grade reading program at Lane High School. *Virginia Journal of Education*, 1948, *41*, 254-255.

Meeks, J.W. Embedded aids to readers: An alternative textbook approach. *Reading Improvement*, 1979, *16*, 95-98.

Memory, D.M. An extended comparison of adjunct aids with low-average and good readers in the sixth grade. *Journal of Educational Research*, 1981, *74*, 405-410.

Memory, D.M. Main idea prequestions as adjunct aids with good and low-average middle grade readers. *Journal of Reading Behavior*, 1983, *12*, 37-48.

Midgett, J., Thompson, R., and Walters, M.J. An investigation of the effectiveness of CAI learning using a tutorial model for teaching interpretive reading comprehension skills to fifth graders. *Florida Reading Quarterly*, 1985, *21*, 21-23.

Miles, D.H. Can the high-school pupil improve his reading ability? *Journal of Educational Research*, 1926, *14*, 88-98.

Miller, G.A. A technique for developing comprehension of literature. *English Journal*, 1934, *23*, 810-818.

Mills, H.C., and Ekert, R.E. An evaluation of reading as a unit in a "how to study" course. *School and Society*, 1934, *40*, 261-264.
Monroe, W.S., and Engelhart, M.D. The effectiveness of systematic instruction in reading verbal problems in arithmetic. *Elementary School Journal*, 1933, *33*, 377-381.
Moore, H. Training college freshmen to read. *Journal of Applied Psychology*, 1934, *10*, 631-634.
Morse, J.M. Effect of reader-generated questions on learning from prose. In W.D. Miller and G.H. McNinch (Eds.), *Reflections and investigations on reading*. Twenty-Fifth Yearbook of the National Reading Conference. Clemson, SC: National Reading Conference, 1976, 310-316.
Neville, D.D., and Hoffman, R.R. The effect of personalized stories on the cloze comprehension of seventh grade retarded readers. *Journal of Reading*, 1981, *24*, 275-278.
Newlun, C.O. *Teaching children to summarize in fifth grade history*, Contributions to Education No. 404. New York: Teachers College, Columbia University, 1930.
Ninth Year Committee for the Walton High School. A reading experiment. *High Points*, 1957, *39*, 12-31.
Nutterville, C., and Bloom, A.Z. The remedial-reading program in Butte High School. *School Review*, 1940, *48*, 428-436.
Oliver, M.E. The effect of high intensity practice on reading comprehension. *Reading Improvement*, 1973, *10*, 16-18.
Olson, A.V., Sanford, A., and Ohnmacht, F. Effectiveness of a freshman reading program. *Journal of Reading*, 1964, *8*, 75-83.
Orlando, V.P., and Hayward, K.G. A comparison of the effectiveness of three study techniques for college students. In P.D. Pearson and J. Hansen (Eds.), *Reading: Disciplined inquiry in process and practice*. Twenty-Seventh Yearbook of the National Reading Conference. Clemson, SC: 1978, 242-245.
Orr, D.B. Retention in educable mentally retarded children of material presented by simultaneous reading and listening. In J.A. Figurel (Ed.), *Forging ahead in reading*. Newark, DE: International Reading Association, 1968, 447-453.

O'Shea, L.J., Sindelar, P.T., and O'Shea, D.J. The effects of repeated readings and attentional cues on reading fluency and comprehension. *Journal of Reading Behavior*, 1985, *17*, 129-142.

Owens, A.M. Generative and passive questions in learning from text. *Perceptual and Motor Skills*, 1980, *51*, 714.

Palincsar, A.S., and Brown, A.L. Reciprocal teaching of comprehension fostering and comprehension activities. *Cognition and Instruction*, 1984, *1*, 117-175.

Paris, S.G., and Jacobs, J.E. The benefits of informed instruction for children's reading awareness and comprehension skills. *Child Development*, 1984, *55*, 2083-2093.

Patching, W., Kameenui, E., Carnine, D., Gersten, R., and Colvin, G. Directed instruction in critical reading skills. *Reading Research Quarterly*, 1983, *18*, 406-418.

Persons, G.L. Silent reading with first-term pupils in the Theodore Roosevelt High School. *High Points in the Work of the High Schools of the City of New York*, 1934, *16*, 5-15. Also reported as A study of silent reading. *English Journal*, 1936, *25*, 33-40.

Pflaum, S.W., and Pascarella, E.T. Interactive effects of prior reading achievement and training in context on the reading of learning-disabled children. *Reading Research Quarterly*, 1980, *16*, 138-158.

Proger, B.B., Carter, C.E., Jr., Mann, L., and Taylor, R.G., Jr. Advance and concurrent organizers for detailed verbal passages used with elementary school pupils. *Journal of Educational Research*, 1973, *66*, 451-456.

Proger, B.B., Taylor, R.G., Mann, L., Coulson, J.M., and Bayuk, R.J. Conceptual pre-structuring for detailed verbal passages. *Journal of Educational Research*, 1970, *64*, 28-34.

Prosser, G.V. The role of relevant active questions in learning based upon successive presentations. *Instructional Science*, 1978, *7*, 359-383.

Ramsey, W.Z. An experiment in teaching reading in high school English classes. *English Journal*, 1957, *46*, 495-500.

Rankin, E.F., Haase, A.M., Stewart, A., and Howard, E. The effect of a sequence strategy on teaching reading comprehension with the cloze procedure. In M.L. Kamil and A.J. Moe (Eds.), *Perspectives on reading research and instruction*. Twenty-Ninth Yearbook of the National Reading Conference. Washington, DC: National Reading Conference, 1980, 201-206.

Raphael, T.E., and McKinney, J. An examination of fifth- and eighth-grade children's question-answering behavior: An instructional study in metacognition. *Journal of Reading Behavior*, 1983, *15*, 67-86.

Raphael, T.E., and Wonnacott, C.A. Heightening fourth grade students' sensitivity to sources of information for answering comprehension questions. *Reading Research Quarterly*, 1985, *20*, 282-296.

Rashotte, C.A., and Torgesen, J.K. Repeated readings and reading fluency in learning disabled children. *Reading Research Quarterly*, 1985, *20*, 180-188.

Raygor, A.L., and Summers, E.G. A comparison of two methods of teaching reading comprehension to high school and college students. In R.C. Staiger and C.Y. Melton (Eds.), *New developments in programs and procedures for college-adult reading*. Twelfth Yearbook of the National Reading Conference. Milwaukee, WI: National Reading Conference, 1963, 118-123.

Readence, J.E., Baldwin, R.S., and Head, M.H. Teaching young readers to interpret metaphors. *The Reading Teacher*, 1987, *40*, 439-443.

Reed, E.E. Improving comprehension through study of syntax and paragraph structure in seventh grade English classes. In J.A. Figurel (Ed.), *Forging ahead in reading*. Newark, DE: International Reading Association, 1968, 575-579.

Rehder, L.G. Reading skills in a paperback classroom. *Reading Horizons*, 1980, *21*, 17-21.

Report on remedial reading. Unpublished Report of a Secondary School Program Conducted in New York City by the Board of Education and the Works Projects Administration, 1939.

Reutzel, D.R. Effectiveness of adjunct story frames on children's reading comprehension. *Reading Improvement*, 1984a, *21*, 182-188.

Reutzel, D.R. Story mapping: An alternative approach to comprehension. *Reading World*, 1984b, *24*, 18-25.

Reutzel, D.R. Story maps improve comprehension. *The Reading Teacher*, 1985, *38*, 400-404.

Rhoades, L.C. Systematic remedial training for pupils of superior reading ability. *Elementary School Journal*, 1929, *29*, 771-773.

Rhodes, E.N. Technique of teaching silent reading. *Elementary School Journal*, 1922, *23*, 296-302.

Richmond, B. The effect of orienting materials in identifying supporting ideas by retarded and normal subjects. *Journal of Research and Development in Education*, 1973, *6*, 155-159.

Rickards, J.P. Type of verbatim question interspersed in text: A new look at the position of effect. *Journal of Reading Behavior*, 1976, *8*, 37-45.

Rickards, J.P., and DeVesta, F.J. Type and frequency of questions in processing textual material. *Journal of Educational Psychology*, 1974, *66*, 354-362.

Rickards, J.P., Anderson, M.C., and McCormick, C.B. Processing effects of common-word and number questions inserted in reading materials. *Journal of Educational Research*, 1976, *69*, 274-277.

Rinehart, S.D., Stahl, S.A., and Erickson, L.G. Some effects of summarization training on reading and studying. *Reading Research Quarterly*, 1986, *21*, 422-438.

Ripple, R.E. Comparisons of the effectiveness of a programed text with three other methods of presentation. *Psychological Reports*, 1963, *11*, 227-237.

Risko, V.J., and Alvarez, M.C. Thematic organizers: Application to remedial reading. In G.H. McNinch (Ed.), *Reading research to reading practice*. Third Yearbook of the American Reading Forum. Athens, GA: University of Georgia, 1981, 119-122.

Ritchie, P. The effects of instruction in main idea and question generation. *Reading-Canada-Lecture*, 1985, *3*, 139-146.

Roberts, B.E., and Stone, C.R. Merits of different plans of training in silent reading. *Educational Method*, 1929, *9*, 155-165.

Roller, C.M., and Schreiner, R. The effects of narrative and expository organizational instruction on sixth grade children's comprehension of expository and narrative prose. *Reading Psychology*, 1985, *6*, 27-42.

Rose, H. Report of three semesters of voluntary reading improvement courses at the University of Kentucky. *Journal of Reading*, 1964, *8*, 126-129.

Roser, N., and Juel, C. Effects of vocabulary instruction on reading comprehension. In J.A. Niles and L.A. Harris (Eds.), *New inquiries in reading research and instruction*. Thirty-First Yearbook of the National Reading Conference. Rochester, NY: National Reading Conference, 1982, 110-118.

Rucker, B.W. Magazines and teenage reading skills: Two controlled field experiments. *Journalism Quarterly*, 1982, *59*, 28-33.

Rudolf, J.B. *The effect of reading instruction on achievement in eighth grade social studies*, Contributions in Education No. 945. New York: Bureau of Publications, Teachers College, Columbia University, 1949.

Sachs, A. The effects of three prereading activities on learning disabled students' reading comprehension. *Learning Disability Quarterly*, 1983, *6*, 248-251.

Salisbury, R. A study of the transfer effects of training in logical organizations. *Journal of Educational Research*, 1934, *38*, 241-254. Also reported as Some effects of training in outlining. *English Journal*, 1935, *24*, 111-116.

Sallee, E.R. Effects of adding folklore to basal reading instruction. *The California Reader*, 1983, *16*, 11-14.

Sallee, E.R., and Sethi, R.R. Effects of adding folklore to basal reading programs. *Reading Horizons*, 1984, *25*, 31-37.

Sampson, M.R., Valmont, W.J., and Allen, R.V. The effects of instructional cloze on the comprehension, vocabulary, and divergent production of third-grade students. *Reading Research Quarterly*, 1982, *17*, 389-399.

Sayre, H.M. Teaching reading in the current events class. *Journal of Educational Research*, 1940, *33*, 561-568.

Schnell, T.R., and Rocchio, D.J. A comparison of underlying strategies for improving reading comprehension and retention. *Reading Horizons*, 1978, *18*, 106-109.

Schneyer, J.W. Use of the cloze procedure for improving reading comprehension. *The Reading Teacher*, 1965, *19*, 174-179.

Schustack, M.W., and Anderson, J.R. Effects of analogy to prior knowledge on memory for new information. *Journal of Verbal Learning and Verbal Behavior*, 1979, *18*, 565-583.

Seaton, H.W., and Wielan, O.P. A study of the effects of listening/reading transfer on four measures of reading comprehension. In G.H. McNinch (Ed.), *Comprehension: Process and product*. First Yearbook of the American Reading Forum. Athens, GA: University of Georgia, 1981, 106-107.

Sebesta, S.L., Calder, J.W., and Cleland, L.N. A story grammar for the classroom. *The Reading Teacher*, 1982, *36*, 180-184.

Seidman, G.M. The effects of previewing and the structured overview on the comprehension of sixth grade children. *Florida Reading Quarterly*, 1984, *20*, 14-16.

Sheldon, S.A. Comparison of two teaching methods for reading comprehension. *Journal of Research in Reading*, 1984, *7*, 41-52.

Sheldon, W. An evaluation of an experimental reading program for medical students. *Journal of Educational Psychology*, 1948, *39*, 298-303.

Shikanai, N. The effects of summarising, note-taking and underlining activities on the learning of prose material. *The Science of Reading* (English summary), 1980, *24*, 1-9.

Shoop, M. Improving inferential comprehension of content by combining instructional techniques. *Reading Improvement*, 1982, *19*, 268-273.

Short, E.J., and Ryan, E.B. Metacognitive differences between skilled and less skilled readers: Remediating deficits through story grammar and attribution training. *Journal of Education Psychology*, 1984, *76*, 225-235.

Siedow, M.D., and Fox, B.J. Effects of training on good and poor readers' use of top-level structure. *Reading World*, 1984, *23*, 340-346.

Simpson, R.G. The effect of specific training on ability to read historical materials. *Journal of Educational Research*, 1929, *20*, 343-351.

Sinatra, R.C., Stahl-Gemake, J., and Berg, D.N. Improving reading comprehension of disabled readers through semantic mapping. *The Reading Teacher*, 1984, *38*, 22-29.

Singer, H., and Donlan, D. Active comprehension: Problem-solving schema with question generation for comprehension of complex short stories. *Reading Research Quarterly*, 1982, *17*, 166-186.

Sjostrom, C.L., and Hare, V.C. Teaching high school students to identify main ideas in expository text. *Journal of Educational Research*, 1984, *78*, 114-118.

Slama, E.A. A silent reading poster lesson. *Chicago Schools Journal*, 1923, *6*, 142-144.

Slater, W.H. Teaching expository text structure with structural organizers. *Journal of Reading*, 1985, *28*, 712-718.

Slater, W.H., Graves, M.F., and Piche, G.L. Effects of structural organizers on ninth-grade students' comprehension and recall of four patterns of expository text. *Reading Research Quarterly*, 1985, *20*, 189-202.

Smith, A.E. The effectiveness of training students to generate their own questions prior to reading. In P.L. Nacke (Ed.), *Diversity in mature reading: Theory and research*. Twenty-Second Yearbook of the National Reading Conference, volume 1. Boone, NC: National Reading Conference, 1973, 71-77.

Smith, E.L. Use of pre-outline organizer in reading textbook assignments. In P.L. Nacke (Ed.), *Diversity in mature reading: Theory and research*. Twenty-Second Yearbook of the National Reading Conference, volume 1. Boone, NC: National Reading Conference, 1973, 83-85.

Smith, R.J., and Hesse, K.D. The effects of pre-reading assistance on the comprehension and attitudes of good and poor readers. *Research in the Teaching of English*, 1969, *3*, 166-176.

Smith, S.D., Slate, D., and Morelock, B. The effects of integrating language and spelling lessons with reading instruction on third grade students' achievement in vocabulary and reading. In G.H. McNinch (Ed.), *Comprehension: Process and product*. First Yearbook of the American Reading Forum. Athens, GA: University of Georgia, 1981, 70-72.

Soltis, J.M., and Pflaum, S. The effect of instruction in connectives on reading comprehension. *Reading World*, 1979, *19*, 179-184.

Speigel, D.L., and Fitzgerald, J. Improving reading comprehension through instruction about story parts. *The Reading Teacher*, 1986, *39*, 676-682.

Spring, C., Blunden, D., and Gatheral, M. Effect on reading comprehension of training to automaticity in word-reading. *Perceptual and Motor Skills*, 1981, *53*, 779-786.

Springsteed, C.B. Improving speed and comprehension in reading. *Journal of Educational Method*, 1925, *5*, 48-52.

Stahl, S. Differential word knowledge and reading comprehension. *Journal of Reading Behavior*, 1983, *15*, 33-50.

Stevens, K.C. Can we improve reading by teaching background? *Memory and Cognition*, 1981, *9*, 142-148.

Stone, C.W. Improving the reading ability of college students. *Journal of Educational Method*, 1922, *2*, 8-23.

Stone, C.W., and Colvin, C. "How to study" as a source of motive in educational psychology. *Journal of Educational Psychology*, 1920, *11*, 348-354.

Stordahl, K.E., and Christensen, C.M. The effect of study techniques on comprehension and retention. *Journal of Educational Research*, 1956, *49*, 561-570.

Straw, S.B., and Schreiner, R. The effect of sentence manipulation on subsequent measures of reading and listening comprehension. *Reading Research Quarterly*, 1982, *17*, 339-352.

Swalm, J., and Cox, G. A content approach to reading skill development for special admit freshmen in a four year college. In F.P. Greene (Ed.), *College reading: Problems and programs of junior and senior colleges*. Twenty-First Yearbook of the National Reading Conference. Milwaukee, WI: National Reading Conference, 1972, 42-49.

Swenby, C., and Zielsdorf, M. A remedial-reading program in a senior high school. *School Review*, 1951, *59*, 350-357.

Swenson, I., and Kulhavy, R.W. Adjunct questions and the comprehension of prose by children. *Journal of Educational Psychology*, 1974, *66*, 212-215.

Taub, H.A. Underlining of prose material for elderly adults. *Educational Gerontology*, 1984, *10*, 401-405.

Taylor, B.M. Teaching middle-grade students to read for main ideas. In J.A. Niles and R.V. Lalik (Eds.), *Solving problems in literacy: Learners, teachers, and researchers*. Thirty-Fifth Yearbook of the National Reading Conference. Rochester, NY: National Reading Conference, 1986, 99-104.

Taylor, B.M. Text structure and children's comprehension and memory for expository material. *Journal of Educational Psychology*, 1982, *74*, 323-340.

Taylor, B.M., and Beach, R.W. The effects of text structure instruction on middle-grade students' comprehension and production of expository text. *Reading Research Quarterly*, 1984, *19*, 134-146.

Thompson, W.H. An experiment in remedial reading. *School and Society*, 1931, *34*, 156-158.

Tillema, H. Webteaching: Sequencing of subject matter in relation to prior knowledge of pupils. *Instructional Science*, 1983, *12*, 321-332.

Tonjes, M.J. Using advance organizers to enhance the processing of texts. In L.J. Chapman (Ed.), *The reader and the text*. Portsmouth, NH: Heinemann, 1981, 131-140.

Traxler, W.H. An experiment in teaching corrective reading to eight seventh-grade pupils. *Journal of Educational Research*, 1935, *29*, 247-253.

Tuinman, J.J., and Brady, M.E. How does vocabulary account for variance on reading comprehension tests? A preliminary instructional analysis. In P.L. Nacke (Ed.), *Interaction: Research and practice for college-adult reading*. Twenty-Third Yearbook of the National Reading Conference. Clemson, SC: National Reading Conference, 1974, 176-184.

Vacca, R.T. The study of holistic and subskill instructional approaches to reading comprehension. *Journal of Reading*, 1980, *23*, 512-518.

Varnhagen, C.K., and Goldman, S.R. Improving comprehension: Causal relations instruction for learning handicapped learners. *The Reading Teacher*, 1986, *39*, 896-904.

Vaughan, J.L., Castel, G., Gilbert, K., and Love, M. Varied approaches to preteaching vocabulary. In J.A. Niles and L. A.

Harris (Eds.), *New inquiries in reading research and instruction*. Thirty-First Yearbook of the National Reading Conference. Rochester, NY: National Reading Conference, 1982, 94-98.

Wagner, M.E. Improving reading ability of high school juniors. *School and Society*, 1932, *36*, 767-768.

Walcott, F.G. New methods and objectives in teaching dull-normal pupils to read. *School Review*, 1936, *44*, 348-361.

Walker, F.R. Evaluation of three methods of teaching reading, seventh grade. *Journal of Educational Research*, 1961, *54*, 356-358.

Wallach, M., and Wallach, L. Helping disadvantaged children learn to read by teaching them phoneme identification skills. In L.B. Resnick and P.A. Weaver (Eds.), *Theory and practice of early reading*. Hillsdale, NJ: Erlbaum, 1979, 197-215.

Westover, F.L. *Controlled eye movements versus practice exercises in reading*, Contributions to Education No. 917. New York: Bureau of Publications, Teachers College, Columbia University, 1946.

White, C.V., Pascarella, E.T., and Pflaum, S.W. Effects of training in sentence construction on the comprehension of learning disabled children. *Journal of Educational Psychology*, 1981, *73*, 697-704.

Wiesendanger, K.D., and Wollenberg, J.P. Prequestioning inhibits third graders' reading comprehension. *The Reading Teacher*, 1978, *31*, 892-895.

Wilhite, S.C. Prepassage questions: The influence of structural importance. *Journal of Educational Psychology*, 1983, *75*, 234-244.

Willey, D.S., and Thomson, C.W. Effective reading and grade-point improvement with college freshmen. *School and Society*, 1956, *83*, 134-135.

Williams, C., and McCabe, M. Improvement of reading ability in a fourth grade class. *Chicago Schools Journal*, 1923, *6*, 54-56.

Williams, K. Effects of text feature instruction on comprehension of original and adapted story versions. In J.A. Niles and R.V. Lalik (Eds.), *Solving problems in literacy: Learners, teachers, and researchers*. Thirty-Fifth Yearbook of the National Reading Conference. Rochester, NY: 1986, 105-108.

Williams, M., and Stevens, V.M.R. Understanding paragraph structure. *Journal of Reading*, 1972, *15*, 513-516.

Winne, P.H. Training students to process text with adjunct aids. *Instructional Science*, 1983, *12*, 243-266.

Wiseman, D.E., Hartwell, L.K., and Kannafin, M.J. Exploring the reading and listening skills of secondary mildly handicapped students. *Learning Disability Quarterly*, 1980, *3*, 56-61.

Witty, P.A., and Lehman, H.C. Teaching the college student "how to study" education. *Education*, 1927, *48*, 47-56.

Wixson, K.K. Vocabulary instruction and children's comprehension of basal stories. *Reading Research Quarterly*, 1986, *21*, 317-329.

Wolf, A.E., and Mikulecky, L.E. Effects of uninterrupted sustained silent reading and of reading skills instruction on changes in secondary students' reading attitudes and achievement. In P.D. Pearson and J. Hansen (Eds.), *Reading: Disciplined inquiry in process and practice*. Twenty-Seventh Yearbook of the National Reading Conference. Clemson, SC: National Reading Conference, 1978, 226-228.

Wong, B.Y.L., and Jones, W. Increasing metacomprehension in learning disabled and normally achieving students through self-questioning training. *Learning Disability Quarterly*, 1982, *5*, 228-240.

Wright, L.B. The value of a motivated assignment: An experiment in directed study. *University of Pittsburgh School of Education Journal*, 1929, 64-67.

Yoakam, G.A. The effect of a single reading. In G.M. Whipple (Ed.), *Report of the society's committee on silent reading*. Twentieth Yearbook of the Society for the Study of Education, Part 2. Bloomington, IL: Public School Publishing, 1921, 90-102.

Yoakam, G.A., and Truby, C. The effects of certain practice exercises in reading. *University of Pittsburgh School of Education Journal*, 1926, *1*, 60-61.